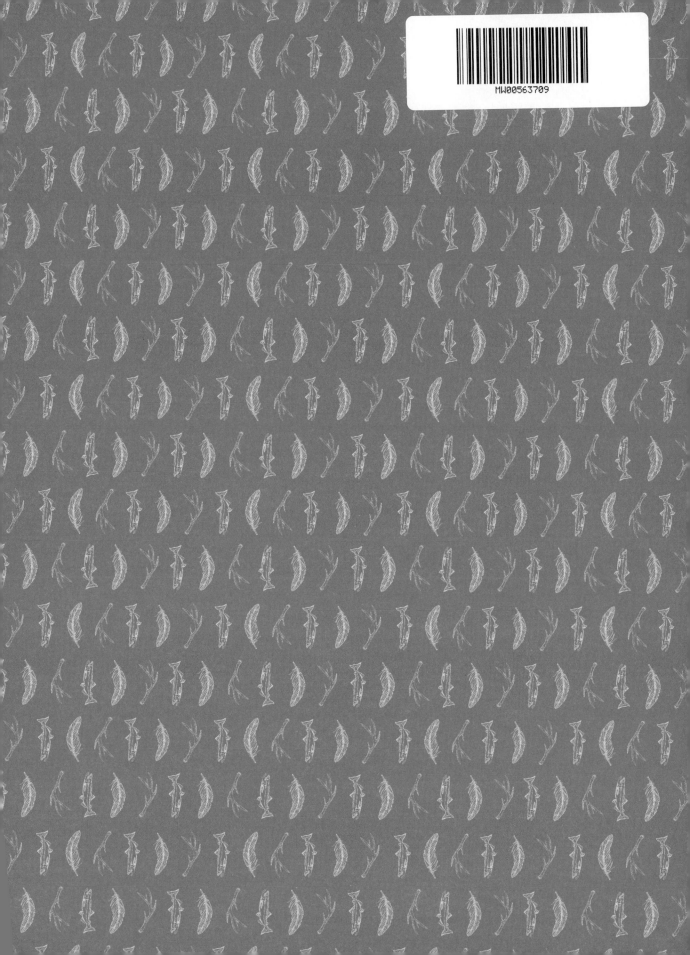

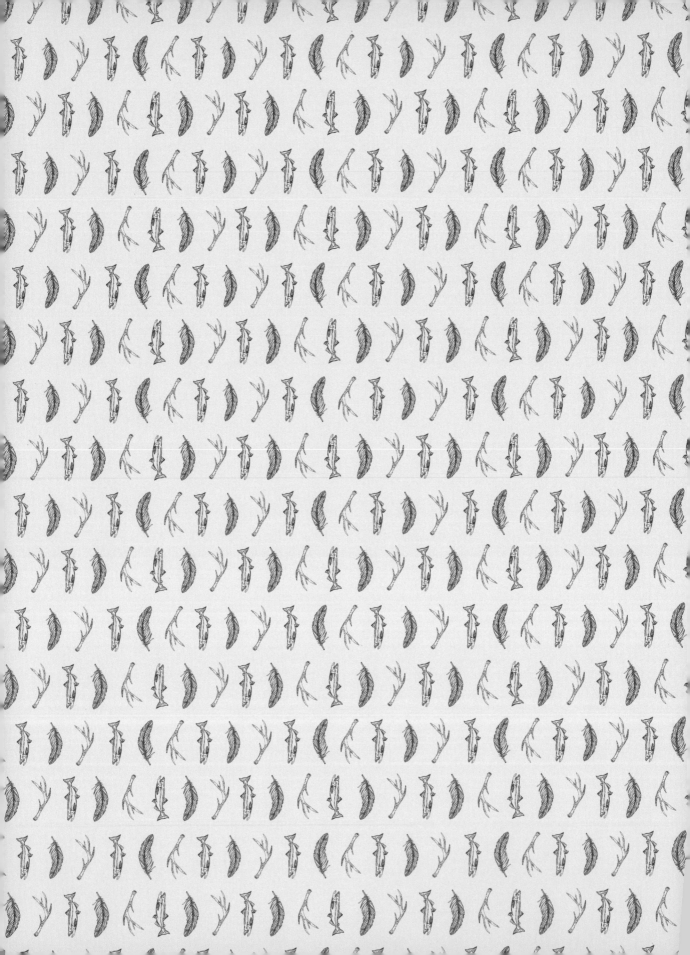

GAME

The Chef's Field to Table Cookbook

A collection of recipes, stories, and possibilities

FROM THE EDITORS OF *COVEY RISE* MAGAZINE

Foreword by Chris Hastings

welcome BOOKS

CONTENTS

TYLER SHARP

TO THE HOPE

Foreword | Chef Chris Hastings

As a chef, outdoorsman, conservationist, and longtime supporter and fan of *Covey Rise* magazine, I jumped at the opportunity to share my thoughts with you on hunting—particularly wild birds, in wild places, from a number of perspectives—and my hope for this cookbook.

From an early age, cooking game has been a large part of my life. I am committed to using as much of my harvest as I can in my everyday cooking, and I take great pains to handle the game correctly, from the initial processing of plucking the feathers or hanging the meat to the final preparation. I also make sure that if I don't use all of the meat the day that I harvest it, I preserve it correctly for later use.

I believe we all face this dilemma from time to time: what to do with our harvest and the importance of our responsibility to honor the life we take. As a young chef, I was taught never to waste anything. It was disrespectful and arguably a sin. If we were lucky, we all learned that same lesson when we were young, from our hunting and fishing mentors. The recipes, tips, and techniques in this cookbook will answer some of the questions often asked about game preparation, and that will allow you greater range in your cooking. But this cookbook is about more than just meals. It's also about the camaraderie that comes from days afield with family and friends and harvesting your own food.

A few years ago, I had the privilege of joining the *Covey Rise* team on assignment at Ruggs Ranch in Heppner, Oregon. You can read more about that experience in "American Idyllic" on page 56. We spent the day foraging for native edibles—including reindeer moss and morels—and hunting wild birds on horseback. I later prepared a meal from the harvest we gathered that day. This truly exemplifies field-to-table cooking, in its purest form. I spent time prepping for the trip in advance to make sure that I was preparing the meal with the freshest, truest ingredients from that area. I took the time to talk to chefs and friends from that region to see what edibles were in season and what I should look for. These experiences are so important to me because I relish the chance to meet new people, taste unique foods, follow a brace of bird dogs, and really enjoy and experience nature around me.

I want to share a few ways you can prep for your own field-to-table experiences. First, traveling to new or familiar places to hunt with friends starts by doing a little work in advance, and paying attention to where you are in any given season. Next, knowing where the flora, fauna, and natural edibles are in their cycles—during those moments your boots grace that ground—will inform your thinking. Obtaining local knowledge from foragers on what options you have to incorporate wild edibles to your meals will also inform your thinking. You can also speak with camp cooks or local chefs about unique food traditions, the availability of prepared foods, and seasonal fruits and vegetables that can be sourced to add to the larder that will complement the different game species you will harvest and cook. You will make the food you prepare unique and create more than just meals by thoughtfully harnessing places you've been, seasons, and memories.

In the pages of this book, I share with you a few recipes prepared on our trip to Ruggs Ranch, including Chukar Heart and Liver Toast (page 43), and a few others such as Grilled Wild Turkey Breast with Grilled Vegetables and Sauce Gribiche (page 192). Because of its simplicity, the Grilled Whole Chukar is my favorite recipe (page 188). It represents my fundamental approach to cooking wild birds. When possible, I cook my birds with the bones in them, because it adds a different level of flavor, and I add only simple ingredients like olive oil and lemon.

In these pages recipes are shared, as well as various techniques—from myself and other chefs—for cleaning and cooking wild game that will take your culinary skills to the next level. The ideas, recipes, and game we cook bind us together in a shared experience: from pitching in on the prep in advance of breaking bread, to sitting around a fire, sipping a delicious beverage, or just enjoying the appetizing fruits of our harvest. All this leads to a hearty meal and stories from the day's adventure. *All of these binding moments.*

I know this cookbook will hold a special place at camp, in your kitchen, and in your life. I also know this: while we follow seasons as outdoorsmen, the true Holy Grail of hunting—the platter that serves us happiness, eternal youth, and sustenance in infinite abundance—is recognizing commitment to, and living in, the often brief moments that nature gives us within those seasons. Those who slow down, take a closer look, and who embrace both this idea and the hope of it will find deeper meaning in the outdoors.

TOP: Built specifically for The Swamp Supper. The first shed was utilized for frying and the second for serving food.

ABOVE: F.D. Stallworth, Sr.,"Granddaddy," sitting on the steps of the old camphouse at The Swamp.

THE SWAMP SUPPER

Introduction | John Thames, Editor-in-Chief and Publisher of Covey Rise *magazine*

I'm not quite sure when the spark ignited this fire inside of me, but as long as I can remember, I have been drawn to the kitchen. I don't know whether it was just to smell the aroma of a meal being prepared or to watch food come to life. Nonetheless, I have many childhood memories of standing and watching different people whip up a quick dish or spend endless hours chopping and mixing for a five-course meal. Growing up in south Alabama, too, probably had a little something to do with why I enjoy food as much as I do.

When I began the process of laying out the design and flow of *Covey Rise* magazine, I wanted to include all the things that made my childhood and life outdoors so memorable and fun. One key ingredient had to be food. A few others were spending time with friends, family, and bird dogs, enjoying the great outdoors, and of course hunting.

My mother, Jocelyn Thames, is a very large part of the reason why there is a food feature in the magazine. She is known for her party planning and execution, cooking, and her "honey do" lists. The lady knows how to get things done. She is the reason for my love of cooking and fellowship. Every day when I arrived home from school, I would climb off the school bus only to be greeted by my dog Luther and a grocery list. My granddaddy's business owned a grocery store a block away from our house, and I was the designated shopper. I would always have three lists: one for our house, one for my granddaddy's house, and one for my grandma's house. It is safe to say that after a few years of shopping, I knew how to pick out a chicken for the fryer, a roast for Sunday lunch, or have the steaks cut for Friday night supper. I knew where everything was on the shelves, as well as what the ingredients were and what they were used for. Looking back, maybe I should have been a chef!

Most trips to the grocery store were followed by an elaborate party or event planned by my mother. This lady has been hosting parties since long before I graced the earth. Julia Child just thought she knew what she was doing in the kitchen. If I heard my mother say "don't stand in the kitchen" once, I heard it a thousand times. The time spent standing in the kitchen under my mother, smelling and sampling everything from fried chicken and potatoes to pound cake and ice cream, are moments I will cherish forever. These moments brought out my love of people and taught me that a meal is not just a meal, it is a meaningful experience that brings people together.

Another great party planner in my family was my granddaddy, F.D. Stallworth, Sr., although I don't know if that's exactly what he'd call himself. He is responsible for my love of fried fish and all the other game that was harvested at The Swamp, our family hunting property. He instilled in me that if you caught the fish or harvested the game, you cleaned and cooked it, or you gave it to someone who would. Nothing was wasted, from small two-finger-size bluegills and ducks from the creek, to squirrels from the hardwoods and rabbits from the field. Looking back now, I realize my granddaddy was teaching me to honor the game we took.

My granddaddy enjoyed hunting and cooking game so much that he began having an annual squirrel supper with a handful of friends a few years after he purchased the property in 1948. Granddaddy was only 27 years old when The Swamp was purchased and the gatherings began.

Imagine several buddies heading out into the woods to enjoy the great outdoors, then gathering around a campsite to clean what they had harvested: food, fun, and fellowship all had while surrounding a campfire, probably with a good drink in hand. It was a privilege

to experience this same tradition as a child. Some 30 years later, it grew to a gathering of 200 plus. It was a Southern showcase—known to the locals as "The Swamp Supper"—of wild game that brought men and their sons from all over the state.

The flagship dish was the Swamp Stew (page 12). It cooked all day in big, black 30-gallon pots that had to be stirred with boat paddles. What a cool sight for a young boy to behold: watching the making of a stew and then stirring it with a paddle bigger than I was. If you could think of any game meat, you could find it at The Swamp Supper, in the stew, and in many other recipes including Caribou Balls (page 15). The ladies of the town would help too, and prepare all the sides, including sweet potatoes, turnip greens, dressing, and every cake or pie you could think of. Some of these recipes are included on the following pages. The ingredient amounts of these recipes still blow my mind. I guess that's what you get when you have more than 200 mouths to feed.

One of the coolest things about the annual event was the big bonfire. "Big" is an understatement. Throughout the year, we collected giant tree trunks on the property, moving them with skidders, just for the Supper. Once we finished sampling all the good food, we would add all paper products to the fire, and we'd stand around, as all men like to do, and tell hunting stories. As we travel the world gathering content for *Covey Rise*, enjoying the great company of new friends and old, we still end each day around a fire. After we've spent time in the kitchen preparing fresh game, and have enjoyed a fine meal, we always find ourselves back around a campfire, enjoying each other's company while sharing memories and resurfacing old stories from days afield. That is what this lifestyle is truly about.

What you will find in this cookbook is a mix of recipes for every level of home chefs and interests. It's for the experienced chef looking for something unique, the outdoorsman who wants to learn new techniques and tips for cooking his harvest, and even the chef who is new to field-to-table cooking, but wants to give it a try. There are easy go-tos like Trout in Foil with Lemon-Sage Butter (page 233), and more adventurous recipes like Braised Elk Chuck Roast with Puttanesca Sauce (page 82), and the never-fail crowd pleasers like Pheasant Flatbread Pizza (page 176). Readers have called in and told us that the

Flatbread Pizza is a favorite recipe, and they use it over and over again with different types of gamebirds. I hope this cookbook does that for you, that these recipes are launching points for your own creativity for whatever is weighing down your game bag. I also hope you find yourself using this cookbook over and over again, making notes, and trying new ways to cook your wild game.

This cookbook can also be a roadmap during your travels. It's a guide for where to eat and drink on your ventures. When traveling to the UK to enjoy the country shooting experience, stop in at the famous Dukes Hotel and Bar (page 266) for the same martinis Ian Fleming enjoyed while writing James Bond novels in a back corner. If you travel to Asheville, North Carolina for grouse in the fall or fish in the summer, while you're there, stop in at Red Stag Grill, where Chef Scott Ostrander (page 100) puts game on the menu, and he doesn't disappoint.

Let the cookbook also plan out your next hunting trip. I know that I am seeking out a woodcock hunt this season after reading the Ginger Citrus Baked Woodcock recipe (page 161). Use this to model what game you want to harvest and what new experience you might want to have. We've done the work for you, now it's time to enjoy.

From the very first issue of *Covey Rise*, we've realized that this lifestyle we all enjoy doesn't begin and end in the field. You, our readers, have realized that too. I remember wondering if the Chef and Plate section would resonate, and to our delight, you have told us—and some more explicitly—"to never take away the recipe section." We've featured the food and drinks that bring the fellowship of days afield to fruition. We've worked with remarkable chefs, photographers, and writers over these past few years, and now we present you with some of the best game recipes, and bring them straight to your table, now in one book.

I hope that you will enjoy this cookbook as much as the chefs and our staff have enjoyed cooking it up for you, our readers and faithful followers. I can truly tell you that the spark that was started more than 40 years ago by my mother has turned into a bonfire. I take advantage of every opportunity to stand in the kitchen with my mother now to share in those moments of cooking, together. This I know about time with her—and family and friends—in the kitchen, around the table, or by the fire: There is nothing more important than that. ✕

Swamp Stew

F.D. STALLWORTH, SR. | SERVES 200 OR MORE

INGREDIENTS

80 to 100 pounds venison
40 pounds boneless pork
40 pounds boneless stew beef
2 hens
2 turkeys
50 squirrels
More meat (such as fryers,
   pork roast, and beef roast)
6 pounds oleo
1 gallon vinegar
2 gallons catsup
2 gallons tomatoes
25 pounds onions
6 bunches celery
4 bottles hot sauce
2 bottles garlic salt
4 bottles Worcestershire sauce
12 lemons
2 boxes salt
2 large cans black pepper
50 pounds potatoes
20 pounds okra
2 gallons whole kernel corn

Chef's Note: Have on hand three large cast iron pots (25- to 30-gallon size), one pot to keep hot water in and two pots for cooking. You'll need one large pile of oak wood and one small pile of pine wood for your fires. Have plenty of water on hand, at least 100 gallons. One chief cook is needed and four good helpers to cook the stew.

TO PREPARE

1. Prepare the meat: Remove all fat and gristle from the venison. Cut the venison, pork, beef, hens, turkeys, and other meat such as fryers, pork, and beef roast into manageable pieces. Add the squirrels whole.

2. Put 2 pounds of oleo in each pot. Add all meats and cook until tender, adding water if needed. Be sure to stir frequently. Remove all bones and discard.

3. Chop and add vinegar, catsup, tomatoes, onions, celery, hot sauce, garlic salt, Worcestershire sauce, and lemons. Add salt and pepper, to taste. Begin adding the potatoes and okra and cook for an hour or so and then add the corn. Season again with salt and pepper, if needed.

✗ *"About 32 years ago about 8 or 10 of my friends and I would hunt together 'down in the swamp' and then gather around the campfire to cook our kill. This has become a traditional affair. Each year the crowds seem to grow larger. Most of our local people come, as well as many from across the state of Alabama and from surrounding states. At our last supper, our crowd had grown to over 500 people. Everyone who is invited looks forward to good food and fellowship. Much credit is given for these successful suppers."*

—F.D. STALLWORTH, SR. (CIRCA 1980)

TOP: F.D. Stallworth, Sr. at Beatrice Hunting Club in Monroe County, Alabama, for a spring turkey hunt in May 1952.

ABOVE: The Swamp Stew, made of over 200 pounds of wild game, would cook all day in large black pots.

Caribou Balls

F.D. STALLWORTH, SR | SERVES 250

INGREDIENTS

25 pounds caribou meat
25 pounds pork sausage
Salt, to taste
Black pepper, to taste
Garlic powder, to taste

1. Mix equal parts of ground caribou meat and pork sausage. Season with salt, black pepper, and garlic powder to taste.

2. Roll the mixed ground meat into small balls. Place the meatballs on cookie sheets and freeze. After they are frozen, remove the meatballs from the pans and place them in Ziploc bags, returning them to the freezer afterward.

To Serve: Remove the meatballs from the freezer. Fry in a small amount of oil to brown, turning several times until done. Remove with a slotted spoon and drain on paper towels, and enjoy!

✗ *"We would take the caribou and mix it with the pork sausage because it was such a lean meat and would fall apart without it. We'd roll the balls for hours on end, freeze and then cook them. There were several taste tests during this to make sure we got it just right."* —JOHN THAMES

Potato Salad

JOCELYN THAMES | SERVES 100

INGREDIENTS

30 pounds potatoes
4 dozen hard-cooked eggs, chopped
4 large bunches celery, chopped
2 quarts salad pickles, chopped
10 small jars chopped pimento
6 onions, chopped
2 quarts mayonnaise
Two 6-ounce jars mustard
7 to 8 finely chopped bell peppers
Salt, to taste
Pepper, to taste

1. Peel and cube the potatoes. Cook in salted water until tender. Drain well.

2. Combine all other ingredients and mix well. Cool.

✗ *"Early morning (the day of the Swamp Supper) we gathered at my house to make Potato Salad. With our Swamp Supper aprons on, the work began. Billy's mother, Frances Thames (Grandma) would have all of the bell peppers already chopped for us. Great memories."* —JOCELYN THAMES

Lou's Cornbread Muffins

LOU DAILEY | SERVES 200 OR MORE

INGREDIENTS

30 pounds self-rising cornmeal
12 dozen large eggs, beaten
½ gallon cooking oil
6 gallons buttermilk

Stir cornmeal, beaten eggs, oil, and buttermilk together. Mix well and pour into muffin tins. Bake at 400 degrees for 25 minutes.

Turnip Greens

LOU DAILEY | SERVES 100

INGREDIENTS

5 washtubs of fresh picked greens
(about 20 bunches per washtub)
10 gallons of water
1 box salt
25 pieces of salted meat

1. Strip stems from middle of leaves, and wash thoroughly several times, making sure all grit is off leaves.

2. Put the turnips in a large pot of water with salt, or a piece of salted meat or other seasoning.

3. Let the turnip greens come to a boil, keeping in mind that they will shrink while cooking. Continue adding greens after they've all cooked down, also adding more water, if needed, and reduce heat to low. Cook for about two hours or until tender. When done, adjust the seasonings.

✗ *"Lou was my fishing partner and a big part of keeping me out of trouble. She could make the best new potatoes and white sauce. My favorite though, was rabbit and dumplings. No matter what she made, she shared with us. I miss those dishes, but I miss her the most. When it came time to prepare the dishes for The Swamp Supper, Lou was in charge of the cornbread and turnip greens."* —**JOHN THAMES**

F.D. Stallworth, Sr.
(Granddaddy) with
Billy Thames (Daddy)

Lou Dailey

TOP LEFT AND ABOVE: The famous bonfire and
scenes from the Supper.

TOP RIGHT: Daddy Ross, who worked at The
Swamp for years, lighting the fire.

Cheese Straws

BILLY THAMES | YIELDS 2 DOZEN

INGREDIENTS

2 cups Cracker Barrel Extra Sharp
 Cheddar Cheese
½ stick Parkay margarine
1 cup plain flour
1 tablespoon baking powder
⅛ to ¼ teaspoon red pepper

1. Sift dry ingredients together several times. Combine dry ingredients with cheese and margarine. Mix well with your hands. Put through a cookie press. (We use an electric gun called a Super Shooter.)

2. Shoot mix onto an ungreased cookie sheet.

3. Bake at 350 degrees about 22 minutes. Cut into desired lengths, and serve.

✗ *"Billy is the cheese-straw maker! We all love them and really do 'pig out' when he makes them. Every year at Christmas we have them, and the grandchildren think they are the best thing ever. The original recipe was shared with us by my aunt, Freida Williams, who was an excellent cook."* **—JOCELYN THAMES**

Cream Cheese Pound Cake

JOCELYN THAMES | SERVES 14

INGREDIENTS

3 sticks butter
8 ounces cream cheese
3 cups sugar
6 eggs
3 cups plain flour
2 teaspoons baking powder
2 teaspoons vanilla extract

1. Preheat oven to 325 degrees, and grease and flour a 10-inch tube pan.

2. In a large bowl, cream butter and cream cheese until smooth. Add sugar gradually and beat until fluffy.

3. Add eggs one at a time, beating well with each addition. Combine the flour and baking powder and add slowly to blender, being careful not to over mix. Add vanilla.

4. Pour into a 10-inch tube pan. Bake at 325 degrees for 1 hour and 30 minutes.

5. Let cool in pan for about 15 minutes before turning onto rack to cool.

✗ *"This is a favorite of everyone! Billy, Will, and John always take this pound cake on their annual fishing trip to Lousiana."* **—JOCELYN THAMES**

SMALL PLATES

Salads, Starters, and Sides

Cinnamon & Chili-Rubbed Woodcock Salad

CHEF DENNY CORRIVEAU | SERVES 2

INGREDIENTS

6 woodcock or quail, breastbones removed
Wild Cheff Blood Orange Olive Oil
Wild Cheff Cinnamon Chili Blend
Salad mix of baby greens
1 cob of sweet (or butter and sugar)corn, stripped from the cob
¾ cup of fresh cherries, pitted and halved
½ to ¾ cup of crumbled goat cheese (bleu cheese can be substituted)
Vinaigrette Dressing (recipe following)

For the Vinaigrette Dressing

⅓ to ½ cup of walnut oil
1 tablespoon of Wild Cheff Blackberry Balsamic Vinegar
1 teaspoon of Wild Cheff Tuscan Spice Blend
Wild Cheff French Sea Salt
Wild Cheff Black Pepper, to taste

1. Heat up outdoor grill to medium-high heat.

2. Place semi-boneless woodcock on a plate and coat with Wild Cheff Blood Orange Olive Oil on both sides, and then season them with Wild Cheff Cinnamon Chili Spice Blend. Let them rest on plate after the grill heats up.

3. Once the grill is hot, place seasoned woodcock onto grill and turn temperature down to medium heat. Close lid for 1 to 2 minutes and let heat create grill marks on first side of the birds.

4. Flip birds and cook until done. Remove and set on plate while you prepare the salad.

5. To make salad, mix all dressing ingredients well with a whisk until it forms a vinaigrette.

6. Toss greens by hand in large bowl with enough vinaigrette to lightly coat the greens (you don't want the greens too soaked as they will get mushy) and then plate the coated greens.

7. Sprinkle fresh corn onto the greens, followed by cherries and then the goat cheese.

To Serve: Arrange cooked woodcock over salad, and enjoy!

CARL TREMBLAY

Scallion Cornbread Cake with Honey Soy Drizzle and Fried Quail Egg

CHEF RUTHIE LANDELIUS | SERVES 4-5 (YIELDS 8-10 SMALL CAKES)

INGREDIENTS

8 quail eggs

⅛ cup low-sodium soy sauce

3 tablespoons local honey

¼ teaspoon chili garlic paste

1 cup seasoned panko crumbs

1 tablespoon sesame oil

1 bunch Tango leaf lettuce or other curly leaf lettuce, roughly chopped

1½ cups Aunt Jemima buttermilk cornmeal mix

1 cup water

1 egg

1 bunch scallions or green onions, julienned

Vegetable oil, for frying

1. Preheat oven to 350 degrees.

2. In a small saucepan, whisk together soy sauce, honey, and chili garlic paste. Let simmer over low heat to thicken about 10 minutes. Set aside.

3. In a small mixing bowl, toss panko with sesame oil to combine. Pour crumbs onto a baking sheet and toast for 8 to 10 minutes in oven. Remove crumbs and toss with lettuce. Set aside.

4. In a medium mixing bowl, combine cornmeal, water, egg, and scallions. Whisk until smooth. Heat a large iron skillet over medium-high heat. Add 1 to 2 tablespoons vegetable oil and allow to get hot. Slowly ladle ¼ cup of cornmeal mixture into the hot skillet, smoothing it out flat as if making pancakes. You should have room to fit four cakes in the skillet. Let fry for 1 to 2 minutes or until edges turn brown and crispy. Flip cakes over, and fry for another minute or so. Repeat until all batter is gone. Once all cakes are fried, keep them warm in the oven or warming drawer and begin to fry the eggs.

5. Crack the top of each quail egg and carefully peel to open a small hole big enough for the egg to slip out into skillet. In the same hot skillet, quickly fry the quail eggs (sunny-side up or over easy, whichever you prefer) in batches of four.

To Serve: Remove the finished cakes from oven or warming drawer to serving plates. Top each with the Tango lettuce/panko mixture, the fried quail eggs, and the honey soy drizzle. These are best if served immediately.

Kale Salad with Creamy Garlic Thyme Dressing

CHEF JOSEPH LENN | SERVES 4

INGREDIENTS

1 or 2 bunches of kale, ribs removed
2 eggs
2 yolks
2 tablespoons lemon juice
2 teaspoons Dijon mustard
4 cloves roasted garlic
1½ cups olive oil
2 teaspoons fresh thyme, chopped
2 tablespoons of Singing Brook
    Cheese, grated in advance
Croutons (recipe following)

1. Combine eggs, yolks, lemon juice, mustard, and garlic, and blend with an immersion blender.

2. Add oil slowly to emulsify (you may need to add a little water if the mixture becomes too thick). Finish by blending in thyme and cheese. Yields about 1 pint of dressing.

FOR THE CROUTONS

2 cups cornmeal
1 teaspoon baking soda
1 teaspoon baking powder
1 tablespoon salt
2 cups buttermilk
1 egg
2 ounces melted butter
¼ cup chopped olives

1. In a bowl, combine all dry ingredients. In another bowl whisk together the egg and buttermilk.

2. With a rubber spatula, pour the wet ingredients into the dry and gently fold them together. Once incorporated, fold the melted butter and olives into the mix.

3. Pour the mixture on a pre-heated baking sheet and bake at 425 degrees until golden brown, approximately 15 minutes. Remove from the pan and crumble the mixture over the top.

4. Place back on the baking sheet and put it in an oven overnight at the lowest setting possible (no higher than 175 degrees). Once dried, place in food processor and grind until coarsely ground.

To Serve: Remove the ribs from the kale, then wash, dry, and cut into ¼-inch to ½-inch strips. Toss the kale in a bowl with enough dressing to lightly coat the kale. Season salad with salt and black pepper. Divide prepared salad onto four plates and garnish with croutons and grated cheese.

Quail Potstickers with Ponzu Sauce

CHEF RUTHIE LANDELIUS | YIELDS ABOUT 45 POTSTICKERS

INGREDIENTS

Breast meat of 6 fresh quail
4 baby bok choy, rinsed and roughly chopped
4 garlic cloves, peeled and roughly chopped
1 small can water chestnuts, drained
1 tablespoon fresh ginger, roughly chopped
1 bunch green onion, roughly chopped
¼ cup soy sauce
3 tablespoons rice wine vinegar
1 egg
2 tablespoons cornstarch
2 tablespoons sesame oil
2 packages wonton wraps
Sesame oil, for frying quail
2 cups chicken or vegetable broth for steaming
Ponzu Sauce (recipe following)

For the Ponzu Sauce

½ cup soy sauce
½ cup rice wine vinegar
2 teaspoons chili garlic paste
2 stems of fresh green scallions, julienned
½ teaspoon sesame seeds

TO PREPARE

1. Combine all ingredients for the Ponzu Sauce, and set aside.

2. Place bok choy in a food processor and pulse until finely shredded. Remove blade and scoop out bok choy with hands. Squeeze water from the bok choy into the sink, and place in a large bowl.

3. Process the garlic cloves, water chestnuts, ginger, and green onion, and then add them to the bowl of processed bok choy.

4. Rinse out the food processor and process the breast meat from the quail until it is completely ground. Add quail to bowl, then add the soy sauce, rice wine vinegar, egg, cornstarch, and sesame oil, and mix well with hands.

5. Set out a cutting board for a work surface. Lay out five wonton wraps in a row at the top of the board. Repeat three more times underneath the previous row. You should have twenty wraps laid out on the cutting board surface (five across, four down). Fill a small dish with water and place next to cutting board.

6. Working with your hands, place about a teaspoon of quail mixture onto the center of each wrap (over-stuffing will cause wonton to open during cooking). Working with one wonton at a time, dip your index finger into the small dish of water and wet two adjoining sides of wonton. Then, fold opposite corners together and press to seal wonton with dry middle finger to avoid getting wonton wrap wet and sticky. Stack wontons onto a baking sheet lined with parchment paper and set aside.

7. Heat a large nonstick skillet over medium-high heat. Add a good-sized splash of sesame oil and gently push each wonton down, on its bottom, into the pan. Let wontons fry until the bottoms are a golden brown, about 3 to 4 minutes. Then, pour enough broth into the pan to cover the wontons by ¼ of an inch.

8. Cover the pan with lid or foil so the potstickers will steam and cook the quail filling, about 5 to 7 minutes or until all broth has evaporated and potstickers have begun "sticking" to the pan, then remove.

To Serve: Place on a large plate and serve with Ponzu Sauce.

"Back home in Texas, my family and I made these pot stickers just about once a month using pork tenderloin instead of quail. Quail can be a tricky bird to prepare and not overcook. I wanted to deliver a different and unique way to cook the lovely squab. By mixing the meat with other ingredients and letting it marinate in soy and sesame oil, you get a delicious filling that is juicy and tender with a hint of sweetness from the quail meat." **—CHEF RUTHIE LANDELIUS**

TERRY ALLEN

Mozzarella Wrapped with Speck ›

CHEF GIANNI GALLUCCI | SERVES 5

INGREDIENTS

Fresh mozzarella, bocconcini
   or ciliegine shape
5 pieces of thinly sliced speck (can
   substitute prosciutto)
Arugula (enough for 5 servings)
Monini Balsamic Glaze

1. Wrap each mozzarella ball with one piece of speck.

2. Place the five pieces on a baking sheet and place in oven at 400 degrees for approximately 4 minutes.

3. Remove from oven and place over a bed of arugula.

To Serve: Drizzle dish with balsamic glaze, and serve.

🌿 *"If I must spend the rest of my life doing one thing, watching people's reaction to my pizza and enjoyment of my dishes sounds good to me. That is much more satisfying to me than any dollar amount."*

—CHEF GIANNI GALLUCCI

Apple & Sage Chukar Sausage

CHEF DENNY CORRIVEAU | SERVES 2-4

INGREDIENTS

1 pound of boneless chukar
   partridge meat, chopped,
   then ground
1 small Cortland apple, peeled,
   cored, and shredded
1 large organic egg, lightly beaten
2 teaspoons of Wild Cheff
   Sagebrush Spice Blend
¼ teaspoon of Wild Cheff Pie
   Spice Blend
3 teaspoons of Wild Cheff
   Air-Dried Shallots
1 teaspoon of Wild Cheff French
   Sea Salt
¼ teaspoon of fresh ground
   Wild Cheff Black Pepper

1. Stir together all ingredients in a large bowl until combined well. Form the sausage into small patties.

2. Preheat grill fire to medium-hot. Once the grill is ready, place the sausage on a lightly oiled grill rack, turning once, until cooked through, about 5 to 6 minutes.

Chef's Note: The sausage will cook quickly, so for best results, fry in a pan with enough butter and/or olive oil to lightly brown. They can also be quickly grilled, either over a traditional gas/charcoal grill or on a lightly oiled, well-seasoned ridged grill pan. Patties can be grilled one day ahead and reheated in a microwave in just one minute. You can also make these into mini patties or even mini meatballs, for an appetizer, along with a dipping sauce.

MIKE SCHALK

Argentinian-Style Pheasant Tartare with Rye Toast, Capers, Tomato, and Basil Oil

CHEF GRAHAM DAILEY | SERVES 6

INGREDIENTS

1½ pounds pheasant breast, trimmed and finely minced

12 slices rye bread

Olive oil, for brushing

½ cup minced shallots

½ cup chopped capers, plus 2 tablespoons for garnish

4 egg yolks

4 tablespoons Basil Oil plus 2 teaspoons for garnish (recipe following)

2 tablespoons lemon juice, freshly squeezed

1 teaspoon hot sauce

2½ teaspoons chopped thyme

1 tablespoon Kosher salt

½ teaspoon coarsely ground black pepper

2 tablespoons diced fresh tomato, for garnish

6 quail eggs, yolks only

1. Brush the rye bread with the olive oil, and toast until crisp on the outside and slightly soft on the inside. Cut off the crusts, and cut the slices in half diagonally, to form triangles.

2. In a large bowl, combine the pheasant breast, shallots, capers, egg yolks, Basil Oil, lemon juice, hot sauce, thyme, salt, and pepper, and stir until combined. Taste, and adjust seasoning if necessary.

FOR THE BASIL OIL

(yields 2 cups)

4 cups water

2 ounces basil leaves

2 cups olive oil

Kosher salt

1. In a large saucepan, bring the water to a boil over medium-high heat. Add the basil and cook until bright green, about 10 to 20 seconds. Transfer immediately to a bowl of ice water to stop the cooking process, and leave for 1 minute, then drain and pat dry with a kitchen towel.

2. In a blender, combine the basil and oil, and purée until smooth. Pour the oil into a large, fine mesh strainer lined with several layers of cheesecloth, and slowly strain into a bowl.

To Serve: Divide the tartare into six equal portions, and form each into 1-by-2 inch ring molds. Place one tartare and four triangles of toast on each of the six plates, and garnish each with capers, Basil Oil, and diced fresh tomato. Top each tartare with one quail egg.

Eastern Shore Goose Jerky

CHEF DAVID GUAS | SERVES 4-6 (YIELDS 16-20 STRIPS)

INGREDIENTS

2 goose breasts, skinless, sliced
   ¼ inch thick
¾ cup low sodium soy sauce
½ cup water
1 tablespoon red pepper, crushed
¼ cup Sriracha
½ cup honey, clover

1. Add the soy sauce, water, crushed red pepper, Sriracha, and honey into a pot at medium heat, until the honey dissolves. Then reserve until it is at room temperature and is no longer warm.

2. Using a mallet, pound the slices of the goose breast evenly, being careful not to make it too thin—you do not want to it break apart. Add the pounded breasts into the reserved marinade, mix around, then transfer everything to a 1-gallon Ziploc bag. Remove most of the air from the bag, and again agitate. Refrigerate for 8 to 12 hours.

3. Remove meat from the bag, lay out on paper towels, then transfer to the various racks of your dehydrator. Turn on and dry for an hour and a half, then flip all pieces, and continue to dry for another hour and a half to 2 hours, or until desired texture and consistency is reached.

Chef's Note: For the dehydrator needed to make the jerky, I use a simple, single-mode Weston Food Dehydrator.

"This recipe is a great way to clean out the freezer at the end of the season. It also provides great protein and a real physical snack in a cold, Eastern shore goose blind." —CHEF DAVID GUAS

Bradley's Circles

CHEF LESLIE SHEPHERD | YIELDS 100 ROUNDS

INGREDIENTS

1 box Pepperidge Farm puff
   pastry sheets (two tri-fold
   sheets), thawed
6 long smoked sausages, casings
   removed

1. Unfold the pastry sheets onto a lightly floured board. Cut each lengthwise at the folds to make three rectangular pieces.

2. Using a rolling pin, roll each piece out about 1-inch wide. Cut sausage to the same length as the sections of dough, and place one piece of sausage lengthwise on top of each piece of dough.

3. Working with one sheet at a time, using a pastry brush, brush cold water down one long side of the dough. Roll sausage up inside the pastry, slightly overlapping the pastry and pressing the seams to seal the dampened edges.

4. Place completed sausage rolls in the freezer until slightly frozen, about 40 minutes. Remove to a cutting board and cut crosswise into ½-inch rounds. Place back in freezer on baking sheet until completely frozen, then pack in tins with sheets of wax paper between each layer. Keep stored in freezer until needed.

5. To prepare, remove as many rounds as needed, place in nonstick skillet, and cook on low to medium heat until browned on both sides.

To Serve: Serve on a plate with Dijon mustard or Bradley's Jalapeño Honey Mustard.

Chef's Note: I use these often, especially when time is short. Just pop them out of the freezer and into the skillet.

"Bradley's Circles are always a hit. Every evening at the plantation, we have appetizers, and just down the road is Bradley's Country Store. At the store, they make their own pork sausage. The sausage is extremely popular with hunters, so I created the Circles, and they have become the perfect fit."

—CHEF LESLIE SHEPHERD

Lamb Chorizo Albondigas with Mint Chimichurri

CHEF ANTHONY LAMAS | SERVES 5-6 (YIELDS 16 MEATBALLS)

INGREDIENTS

1 pound ground lamb shoulder or leg, proportion of 2 parts lean to 1 part fat
2 tablespoons Kosher salt
2 tablespoons fresh toasted breadcrumbs
1 egg
1 tablespoon ice-cold water
Zest of 2 lemons
Juice of 2 lemons
Seasoning Blend (recipe following)
Mint Chimichurri (recipe following)

For the Seasoning Blend

1 tablespoon fresh minced garlic
1 tablespoon fresh oregano
1 teaspoon smoked paprika
1 teaspoon chili powder
1 teaspoon cayenne pepper
1 teaspoon cumin
1 teaspoon coriander
1 teaspoon black pepper
1 teaspoon crushed red pepper flakes

For the Mint Chimichurri

1 cup spearmint leaves
½ cup fresh parsley
½ cup fresh cilantro
1 teaspoon crushed red pepper
Juice of 1 lemon
1 garlic clove
¼ cup olive oil
¼ cup red wine vinegar
1 tablespoon Kosher salt

1. In a large bowl, mix the meatball ingredients well, and add the seasoning blend. Integrate into the meatball mix, and allow to chill in the refrigerator for 1 hour.

2. For the Mint Chimichurri, purée all ingredients and chill in the refrigerator for a half-hour.

3. Preheat oven to 375 degrees. Roll into 2-ounce meatballs on a baking pan and place in oven for 8 to 10 minutes until browned.

To Serve: Serve on a small plate with Mint Chimichurri.

Crispy Chicken Livers with Sofrito

CHEF ANTHONY LAMAS | SERVES 6-8

INGREDIENTS

1 pound chicken livers
1 quart buttermilk or heavy cream
2 cups flour
1 tablespoon cumin
1 tablespoon coriander
1 tablespoon cayenne
1 tablespoon Kosher salt
1 tablespoon smoked paprika
1 onion, caramelized
Sofrito (recipe following)

For the Sofrito

1 bell pepper
1 tomato
¼ Spanish onion
1 clove garlic
1 teaspoon chopped fresh oregano
¼ cup olive oil
¼ cup red wine vinegar
1 teaspoon achiote (also called annatto)—try the Goya Sazon seasoning
Salt and pepper, to taste

1. Clean chicken livers and cut into 2-inch pieces. Soak livers in buttermilk or heavy cream, refrigerate for at least 1 hour. Remove livers from soak.

2. Combine flour, cumin, coriander, cayenne, salt, and paprika, and toss chicken livers in mixture to heavily coat. Set aside on a plate. Heat canola oil or fryer to 350 degrees. Deep fry or pan fry for 2 minutes. Pull out of oil and set on paper towels to drain for 30 seconds.

3. Add caramelized onions to warm sauté pan over medium heat. Add fried chicken livers to pan and toss together for 30 seconds.

4. Purée sofrito ingredients together in blender. Refrigerate for 1 hour before using.

To Serve: Pour prepared livers into a serving dish, add skewers for serving. Garnish with chopped Italian parsley or fresh oregano and sofrito for dipping.

Salad of Chicories, Apple & Pecans

CHEF STEVEN SATTERFIELD | SERVES 4-6

INGREDIENTS

2 bunches variety chicory greens
   (radicchio, endive, escarole,
   or frisée)
2 small, crisp, sweet-tart apples
   such as Cameo, Mutsu, or
   Limbertwig
1 cup pecan halves
Salt and pepper, to taste
Shallot Vinaigrette (recipe
   following)

1. Roast pecans for 7 to 10 minutes at 300 degrees. If you smell their sweet, nutty scent wafting from the oven, remove immediately. Do not overcook.

2. Trim chicory leaves, removing any thick, woody stems, then wash well, and spin dry in a salad spinner. Run a knife across the leaves in two different directions to cut them into smaller pieces that will fit easier onto your fork.

3. Cut the apples into quarters, exposing the seeds. Turn each quarter cut side down onto a cutting board, with the other cut side facing you and the skin side facing away. Holding your knife at an angle, slice away the seeds at a 45 degree angle. Do this for each quarter, then slice into thin slices, skin side facing towards you, with the new cut facing down towards the cutting board, for stability.

4. In a large bowl, combine the chicory leaves and apples, and season lightly with salt and pepper. Add a few tablespoons of dressing along the inside of the bowl along the edge and then toss to coat. Work the chicory for a full minute with your fingers, massaging until tender.

FOR THE SHALLOT VINAIGRETTE

3 tablespoons finely diced shallots
1 tablespoon Dijon mustard
1 teaspoon salt
7 turns freshly ground black
   pepper
2 tablespoons apple cider vinegar
2 tablespoons sherry vinegar
½ cup pecan oil from Oliver Farm
¼ cup extra-virgin olive oil

Combine shallots, mustard, salt, pepper, and the vinegars together in a small mixing bowl. Stir well to combine, and then slowly drizzle in oils, whisking all the while.

To Serve: Transfer the dressed chicory and apples to a plate or platter and garnish with toasted pecans and the Shallot Vinaigrette.

"What I wanted was to respond to the harvest, meaning what is available now in this season—not just fruits and vegetables, but also dairy, cheeses, oils, and nuts. I used to think my life was eclectic, but now I see the continuous line: Everything I do uses math, science, and creativity."

—CHEF STEVEN SATTERFIELD

Grilled Quail Salad with Strawberries, Aged Balsamic Vinegar, and Marcona Almonds

CHEF GORDON HAMERSLEY | SERVES 4

INGREDIENTS

- 4 quail, dressed and split down the backbone
- 1 teaspoon salt
- ½ teaspoon freshly ground black pepper
- 1 pinch cayenne pepper
- ⅛ teaspoon fennel seeds, crushed
- 4–6 tablespoons aged balsamic vinegar
- 4 tablespoons extra-virgin olive oil
- 1 pint fresh strawberries, washed, stemmed, and cut into ¼-inch slices
- 1 head of baby frisée lettuce, cut, washed, and dried
- 1 cup parsley leaves, washed, dried, and torn into pieces
- 1 fennel bulb, trimmed and cut into very thin julienne slices
- 2 ounces Marcona almonds, roasted and salted

1. In a shallow baking dish, add the salt, black pepper, cayenne pepper, fennel, 1 tablespoon of the aged balsamic vinegar, and 1 tablespoon of extra-virgin olive oil. Stir to combine.

2. Press the quail on a cutting board using your hand to flatten the birds. Place the quail in the baking dish and evenly coat them with the assembled mixture. Let marinate in the refrigerator for about 1 hour, turning once or twice.

3. Place the remaining vinegar and olive oil in a small bowl. Add the strawberries and a pinch of salt and pepper. Let this macerate at room temperature for 1 hour. (Do not leave soaking for more than 90 minutes, as the berries will begin to deteriorate.)

4. Heat the grill. The fire should be moderately hot. Brush the grill grates with a small amount of cooking oil. Lift the quail out of the marinade and pat dry. Grill the quail, breast side down, for about 3 to 4 minutes. Turn the quail and finish the cooking, about 3 to 4 more minutes. If the quail are getting too dark, move them to the side of the grill so they do not burn. When done grilling, remove the quail to a platter or board and let them rest while making the salad.

To Serve: Place the frisée, parsley leaves, and fennel in a salad bowl. Add 2 to 3 teaspoons of the strawberry balsamic mixture and toss well to dress the salad. Divide salad greens among four plates. Remove strawberries from marinade and arrange them around the greens. Place a quail on the greens and drizzle with a little more balsamic dressing. Top with roasted almonds.

Grilled Duck Roulade with Sundried Tomatoes

CHEF ANGELIA HIGHSMITH | SERVES 4

INGREDIENTS

4 duck breasts
Sundried tomatoes in oil,
  julienned
Salt and pepper, to taste
Blackberry Chipotle Barbecue
  Sauce (recipe following)

1. Pound each duck breast out to about ⅛-inch thick, and season each with salt and pepper.

2. Place a generous amount of sundried tomatoes along one side of each breast. Roll up the duck breast, securing each with at least two toothpicks.

3. Take the tomato oil and rub onto outside of the duck breasts.

4. Grill until duck is medium rare over medium-high heat.

FOR THE BLACKBERRY CHIPOTLE BARBECUE SAUCE

(yields approximately 5 cups)
3 cups ketchup
⅔ cup apple cider vinegar
6 tablespoons Worcestershire
½ cup molasses
½ cup honey
7 tablespoons brown sugar
1 teaspoon onion powder
1 teaspoon garlic powder
1 teaspoon salt
1 teaspoon black pepper
1 teaspoon dry mustard
¼ teaspoon liquid smoke
¼ cup blackberry juice
¾ teaspoon ground ginger
¾ teaspoon ground chipotle pepper

Place all ingredients in a saucepan. Bring to a simmer on medium low heat, and cook for at least 30 minutes. Serve sauce on the side next to the duck.

Chef's Note: If you prefer a standard barbecue sauce for this or other dishes, simply leave out the last four ingredients of the barbecue sauce.

Chukar Heart and Liver Toast with Muscadine Jam

CHEF CHRIS HASTINGS | SERVES 4

INGREDIENTS

8 chukar hearts, finely chopped
8 chukar livers, finely chopped
1 tablespoon butter
1 tablespoon extra-virgin olive oil
1 shallot, finely minced
1 teaspoon fresh chopped thyme
2 ounces bourbon
1 tablespoon chopped flat-leaf
   parsley
2 ounces muscadine jam
4 toast points
Salt, to taste
Pepper, to taste

1. In a cast iron skillet or stainless sauté pan, heat butter and olive oil. Add shallots and thyme. Cook slowly for 3 to 4 minutes until shallots are translucent.

2. Turn to high heat and add hearts and liver. Cook for 2 minutes. Add bourbon, flame, and cook for one minute.

3. Remove from heat, and add salt, pepper, and chopped parsley. Brown toast points.

To Serve: Spread ¼ of liver and heart mixture onto each toast point. Place ½ a teaspoon of muscadine jam on toast, and serve.

"While in Oregon at Ruggs Ranch, we prepared Chukar Heart and Liver Toast for the cowboys that were with us. I remember chopping up the hearts and livers, and they could not believe that we were going to eat this. We foraged for reindeer moss and morels earlier that day and were going to eat those as well. They were very turned off to the idea of eating all of this, but once they got over their initial fear and tasted the dish, they were blown away. I love this recipe because it shows that you can eat other parts of the bird besides the breast and the legs." —**CHEF CHRIS HASTINGS**

Smoked Scamp West Indies Salad

CHEF ROB MCDANIEL | SERVES 6

❧ *"Several years ago, I spent a weekend in Bayou La Batre at which time I toured a crab-picking facility and had my first taste of West Indies Salad. To be honest, I didn't think I would like it simply because I knew what was in it. But boy, was I wrong. After that moment, I was in love with how a few simple ingredients could transform a pound of crab so drastically. I like a heavy hand when it comes to the onion and black pepper but I will let you make your own assumptions. You're probably scratching your head by now, as the recipe I have provided is for scamp not crab. Well, let me explain. Crab can be a little pricey, especially if you're trying to feed a crowd, so one day I experimented with smoked white fish. This recipe will work with crab, scamp, sheepshead (one of my favorites), triggerfish, snapper, and even crappie and bream. I hope you enjoy as much as I do."* —**CHEF ROB MCDANIEL**

INGREDIENTS

2½ pounds scamp fillets, skinned and boned
1½ cups brown sugar
1 cup Kosher salt
5 bay leaves
1 teaspoon toasted whole black peppercorns
1 crushed head of garlic
2 cups plus ⅔ cup water
2 small sweet yellow onions, minced
1¼ cup cider vinegar
⅔ cup canola oil
1 tablespoon freshly ground black pepper

1. Place water, brown sugar, Kosher salt, bay leaves, black peppercorns, and garlic in a large nonreactive pot, and simmer until the salt and sugar have dissolved. Remove from heat, and add 2 cups of ice to cool it quickly.

2. Once your brine has cooled to 40 degrees, place into a 1-gallon plastic container with fish fillets, and refrigerate for 6 hours. Drain from brine, pat dry, then spread out in a single layer to air dry for an hour. Remove.

3. Place fillets into a 250-degree smoker for 2 hours. (You want to maintain a low, constant hickory smoke if possible. The time will depend on the thickness of the fillets, which should be white and flaky when done. If your fillets are small and thin, they won't take the entire 2 hours.)

4. Flake the smoked scamp into quarter-sized chunks.

5. In a large nonreactive bowl, combine fish, onions, cider vinegar, canola oil, ⅔ cup of ice water, and ground black pepper. Stir to mix everything well, then place plastic wrap over the top and refrigerate for at least 12 to 24 hours. Gently stir every couple of hours, if possible.

To Serve: Serve chilled with saltine crackers and a cold beer or nice Sancerre.

Chef's Note: The air drying is a very important step, as this allows the fish to form a tacky layer called pellicle. The pellicle layer will allow smoke to penetrate the fish but will also keep the fish from drying out.

Wild Turkey Salad with First of the Season Morels and Watercress

CHEF CHRIS HASTINGS | SERVES 4

INGREDIENTS

Twelve ⅛-inch thick slices wild turkey breast, about 4 to 5 ounces
¼ cup buttermilk
1 tablespoon Dijon mustard
1½ teaspoons Kosher salt, divided
1 teaspoon freshly ground black pepper, divided
3 cups Fresh Breadcrumbs (recipe following)
¼ cup peanut oil, for cooking
1 tablespoon olive oil
1 tablespoon minced shallots
¼ teaspoon chopped fresh thyme
3 ounces fresh morel mushrooms
Pinch of Kosher salt
Pinch of freshly ground black pepper
12 cups (1½ bunches) loosely packed fresh watercress
¼ cup Lemon-Dijon Vinaigrette (recipe following)
2 ounces fresh chèvre, crumbled
2 tablespoons finely chopped fresh chives

1. Combine the buttermilk and the mustard with ½ teaspoon of the salt and ½ teaspoon pepper in a shallow dish. Add the turkey slices, turning to coat. Cover, and allow the turkey to marinate in the refrigerator for 1 hour.

2. Season the breadcrumbs with the remaining teaspoon of salt and ½ teaspoon of pepper. Dredge the turkey slices in the breadcrumbs, pressing to make sure the crumbs adhere to the turkey. Place breaded turkey on a parchment paper-lined plate. (At this point, the turkey can be covered and refrigerated up to 2 hours, if needed.) Just before serving, heat the peanut oil in a large cast iron skillet over medium-high heat until hot. Add the turkey, in batches, and cook 1½ to 2 minutes on each side or until golden brown. Remove from the heat and drain on a paper towel-lined plate. Repeat with remaining turkey slices. Cover to keep warm.

3. To prepare the salad, heat the olive oil in a small skillet over medium-high heat. Add the shallots, thyme, and mushrooms, cook until softened, 4 to 5 minutes. Season the mushrooms with a pinch of salt and remove from the heat. Allow mushrooms to cool for 10 minutes before tossing the salad.

FOR THE FRESH BREADCRUMBS

Several recipes call for fresh breadcrumbs as opposed to dried breadcrumbs. To achieve the correct results, start with a fresh French baguette, torn into 2-inch pieces. Place the bread pieces in a food processor and pulse until the bread forms a uniform crumb consistency. At this point the fresh breadcrumbs can be used immediately or stored in an airtight container in the freezer for up to three months.

FOR THE LEMON DIJON VINAIGRETTE

(yields about 2 cups)
½ cup plus 2 tablespoons fresh squeezed lemon juice
¼ cup Dijon mustard
½ cup olive oil
½ cup extra-virgin olive oil
2 tablespoons finely chopped shallots
2 tablespoons finely chopped fresh parsley
½ teaspoon finely chopped fresh thyme
½ teaspoon Kosher salt
½ teaspoon freshly ground black pepper

Whisk together the lemon juice, mustard, and olive oils. Stir in the shallots, parsley, and thyme. Season the vinaigrette with salt and pepper. Use immediately, or refrigerate until ready to serve.

To Serve: Combine the watercress and the cooled mushrooms in a large bowl with the vinaigrette, tossing until well coated. Layer one-third of the watercress mixture on each of four serving plates. Top each salad with one slice of fried turkey. Repeat the layers two more times. Crumble about ½ ounce of the chèvre goat cheese and ½ tablespoon of the chives over each salad and serve immediately.

Aunt Esta's Dinner Rolls

CHEF BRIAN MERCURY | MAKES 24 ROLLS

 "These are called Aunt Esta's rolls, but she's actually my great aunt. I grew up in a very family-focused atmosphere, always connected to my extended family. It was all blended together, and even though you knew how you were connected, everyone was still Uncle Joe or Aunt Joanne, Cousin Sarah or Andrea. It didn't matter—we were family. I would spend summers visiting my grandma's family in Michigan, which is where Aunt Esta lived, working at my Uncle Junior's pig farm. That is where Aunt Esta's rolls were the best! We made them back in Rochester, New York, where I was from. But there is something about the way Aunt Esta made them...it was special." **—CHEF BRIAN MERCURY**

INGREDIENTS
1 cup water, room temperature
0.8 ounce instant yeast
4 ounces butter, soft
1½ teaspoons salt
6 ounces white sugar
3 eggs
1½ pounds bread flour

1. Combine water and yeast in a mixing bowl and stir to dissolve.

2. With dough hook attachment on mixer, add prepared yeast, butter, eggs, sugar, and salt. Add flour, and mix until smooth dough forms, about 5 minutes.

3. Divide dough into roughly 2¼-ounce portions, and roll into balls. Heavily spray a cast iron pan and place the prepared dough balls in four rows of six rolls each. Cover, and place in refrigerator overnight.

4. Remove rolls from refrigerator and proof in a warm place until rolls have doubled in size, usually 2 to 3 hours.

5. Preheat oven to 325 degrees. Brush rolls with egg wash and bake about 18 to 25 minutes or until golden brown.

6. Remove rolls from the oven, brush with melted butter, and sprinkle lightly with salt and sugar.

Toasted Buckwheat with Grilled Broccolini and Butternut Romesco Sauce

CHEF JOSEPH LENN | SERVES 6

FOR THE BUCKWHEAT

1½ cups buckwheat groats
3 cups vegetable broth
2 teaspoons salt
1 tablespoon minced chives

1. In a medium saucepot over high heat, bring the vegetable broth and salt to a boil, and then add buckwheat groats. Reduce heat to low and cook for 10 minutes.

2. Remove from heat and strain excess liquid. Rinse buckwheat in a strainer and allow all water to drain. Next, place buckwheat on a towel to remove excess moisture, and reserve.

FOR THE ROMESCO SAUCE

(yields 1 quart)
1½ pounds butternut squash
3 red bell peppers
1 dried ancho chili (soaked in water overnight)
3 ounces hazelnuts (toasted)
1 head roasted garlic cloves
Sherry vinegar, to taste
Salt, to taste

1. Cut butternut squash in half. Remove the seeds and season with salt and pepper. Drizzle with a small amount of olive oil and place on a baking sheet, skin side down. Place in 350-degree oven and roast for 45 minutes to 1 hour.

2. While the squash is roasting, prepare the peppers. In a natural wood grill over low heat, place the red peppers on the grill. Char the peppers until the skins are black. Remove and place them in a bowl covered with plastic wrap, and set aside for 20 minutes. Then, remove the charred skins from the red peppers, then remove the stems and seeds.

3. In a food processor, grind hazelnuts fine though not to a paste. To this, add the roasted red peppers, ancho chili, butternut squash, roasted garlic cloves, and process until all is incorporated. Finish with sherry vinegar and salt.

FOR THE BROCCOLINI

2 bunches broccolini (or substitute 1 head of broccoli)
1 tablespoon olive oil
1 teaspoon salt

1. In a large pot over high heat, bring water to a boil. Working in batches, blanch broccolini in boiling water, and shock it in ice water. Remove broccolini from the water and dry with a towel.

2. In a mixing bowl, combine broccolini, olive oil, and salt, and toss until coated.

3. Prepare a natural wood grill. Once the coals are glowing, cover and let the grill cool to medium heat. Place broccolini on the grill and cook over medium heat until brown. Turn broccolini and repeat the process. Once browned, remove from the grill and reserve in a warm spot.

To Serve: In a large nonstick pan over medium-high heat, place 1 tablespoon olive oil into the pan and heat until shimmering. Add buckwheat and toast until brown and crispy. Do not stir the buckwheat too much. Once crispy, remove from heat and stir in the chives. Place 2 tablespoons of Romesco Sauce onto each plate, divide the buckwheat onto the plates, and finish with the reserved broccolini. Serve extra sauce on the side.

Sagebrush & Parmesan Grouse Meatballs

CHEF DENNY CORRIVEAU | SERVES 4

INGREDIENTS

4 boneless grouse breasts, skin removed, about ½ a pound
4 tablespoons of Wild Cheff Blood Orange Olive Oil
½ small onion, diced
2 fresh cloves of garlic, minced
1 teaspoon of pine nuts
1 teaspoon of Wild Cheff Sagebrush Spice Blend
2 tablespoons of Parmesan cheese, freshly grated
1 organic egg, scrambled

1. Place 2 tablespoons of Wild Cheff Blood Orange Olive Oil into medium sauté pan and cook onion, garlic, and pine nuts over medium heat for approximately 5 minutes until onion is softened and cooked. Set aside and cool.

2. Cut grouse into manageable pieces and grind in meat grinder or food processor.

3. Remove ground meat and mix in large bowl with other ingredients.

4. Form meat mixture into ½-inch balls and place on cookie sheet that has been lightly coated with olive oil.

5. Place into preheated 375-degree oven for 15 to 20 minutes. Remove and serve.

Chef's Note: Add small amount of plain breadcrumbs, if mixture is too loose.

Beet and Radish Salad with Orange Vinaigrette

CHEF ROB MCDANIEL | SERVES 4

Chef's Note: Use baby beets, which are sweeter than the larger ones. Use whichever varieties you prefer or can find, but be sure to keep the red beets separate, as they will bleed into the others.

INGREDIENTS

25 baby beets (red, golden, and candy-striped, or Chioggia)
Selection of radishes (watermelon, French Breakfast, cherry belle, black, and lime)
2 cloves garlic
Thyme, to taste
Chili, to taste
Olive oil, to taste
Salt and pepper, to taste
1 bunch Italian flat-leaf parsley, picked clean and chopped small
¼ cup of toasted pecans
4 ounces Belle Chévre cheese (fresh goat cheese can be substituted)
Orange Vinaigrette (recipe following)

1. Season the beets with olive oil, salt, pepper, thyme, garlic, and chili, and roast in a covered roasting pan, about 20 to 40 minutes. Check them with a paring knife after 20 minutes, and then again every 5 minutes, for doneness. When the beets have cooled, peel them using a kitchen towel or paper towel to rub the skins off, keeping the red beets separate, then quarter them and set aside.

2. Using a mandoline, shave the radishes into thin rounds and place them in a bowl of ice water for 5 to 10 minutes. Prepare the parsley by picking it clean of any stems, then chopping small with a kitchen knife. Set aside.

3. Mix together the golden and candy-striped beets, the shaved radishes, chopped Italian parsley, and about 3 tablespoons of the Orange Vinaigrette, adding salt and pepper to taste. In a separate bowl, season the red beets in the same way, using more of the vinaigrette for this, about 1 tablespoon.

FOR THE ORANGE VINAIGRETTE

Pulp from half a vanilla bean
Zest of 2 oranges, peeled and julienned
1 teaspoon minced shallot
6 sprigs of thyme (picked and chopped)
⅓ cup Champagne vinegar
⅓ cup extra-virgin olive oil
1 arbol chili, chopped

1. Scrape the pulp from half a vanilla bean and place in a nonreactive mixing bowl.

2. Using a peeler, peel the zest off of an orange, being careful not to include the white.

3. Julienne the zest into a mixing bowl, and add the shallots, thyme, arbol chili, and vinegar. Let this macerate for 15 minutes; then slowly whisk in the olive oil, and season to taste.

To Serve: Arrange the seasoned salad on a platter or divide among individual serving plates, adding the red beets (which you've reserved until now), adding more vinaigrette if desired. Finish with the Belle Chévre and the toasted pecans.

"The fact that you can talk about where the food came from, who grew it, how it was grown, the process behind it—that's all part of the story of what goes on the plate."
—CHEF ROB MCDANIEL

"Black Powder" Venison Jerky

CHEF CHARLIE PALMER | YIELDS ABOUT 5 POUNDS

INGREDIENTS

6 pounds venison leg meat or
    flank steaks
1 cup sorghum
1½ cups soy sauce
1 tablespoon liquid smoke
¼ cup Worcestershire sauce
2 tablespoons finely ground
    black pepper
1 tablespoon garlic powder
1 tablespoon onion powder

1. Holding a knife blade at a 45-degree angle and slicing diagonally to make a tranche—much as you would slice a side of smoked salmon but at a much less exaggerated angle—cut the meat against the grain into ¼-inch strips.

2. Whisk the sorghum, soy sauce, liquid smoke, Worcestershire sauce, black pepper, garlic powder, and onion powder until well combined, making sure the sorghum is fully dissolved and doesn't sink to the bottom of the bowl. Pour about one-fourth of the mixture into a square-sided, nonreactive container (a Pyrex casserole dish works well). Layer the slices of meat in evenly, and pour more marinade over, as needed, to coat all the pieces equally. Cover and refrigerate for 24 hours.

3. Remove the slices of meat from the container and layer them between paper towels to remove excess marinade. Turn the oven on at the lowest setting. Lay the slices on lightly oiled baking racks, leaving a little space between the pieces so the jerky dries evenly.

4. Place the baking racks directly on the oven racks, without baking sheets or anything else that will block the air and heat from circulating around the oven.

5. Leave the oven door cracked open throughout the drying process, which will take up to 8 hours. Halfway through the drying process, check the progress, flipping the slices of meat and rotating the racks. The jerky is done when it is still slightly pliable but not so dry as to be crisp and breakable.

6. Let the jerky rest at room temperature to allow any moisture left inside the meat to equalize with the drier, outside surface, for about 1 hour. Transfer to an airtight container and store in a cool place. Jerky will keep for up to 2 months, if refrigerated.

AMERICAN IDYLLIC

Story and photography by Tyler Sharp

Drawing from a lifetime of outdoor experience, Chef Chris Hastings prepares locally sourced food that's synced with the seasons, honoring the place and traditions of the past.

As we sat around a campfire in the Blue Mountains of central Oregon, plucking feathers from the chukar we harvested, passing a bottle of Pendleton Whisky among us, Chef Chris Hastings told us about his childhood summers on Pawleys Island in the coastal salt marshes of South Carolina.

"I was the creek boy, and for more than a month each summer, my job was to provide for my family. I relished that task, and the responsibility it held. I would catch fish in the surf, gig flounder at night, jib oysters, net shrimp, and dig for clams. You could catch all the crabs you needed for ten people with some chicken neck, fishing line, and a weight," Chef Hastings told me as deplumed feathers swirled in the mountain breeze. "I learned a lot about the cycles of nature, the ebb and flow of life, certain times of the year when the shrimp are in, or when the redfish are tailing, and what it meant to be on the salt marsh during a full moon," he elaborated as prep continued for the ensuing rustic meal. "You gotta know what moment you're in, get what you can get, take it home, and eat it."

Echoing Robert Ruark's *The Old Man and the Boy*, (Hastings's favorite novel and influence for his own cookbook), it was the salt marshes of South Carolina that first attuned him to nature's rhythms, season by season, teaching him not only how to live off the bounty of the land, but also to revere it.

"If you take a life, you respect the life, and should pay homage to it however you can. I try to do that through my cooking by not wasting any part of the animal," he says. Hastings even makes quill pens from the feathers of turkeys taken in the spring.

One of the more revered chefs in the South, Hastings had little idea how his idyllic youth would come to shape his career and his personal values. A graduate of Johnson & Wales University College of Culinary Arts in Rhode Island, he entered the Birmingham, Alabama, scene under the influential wing of Frank Stitt, who is considered the father of fine dining in the area. It was here that Hastings met his future wife and business partner Idie, and together they moved west to the Bay Area in 1989, where she would earn a degree of her own from the Culinary Institute of California. Under the tutelage of Bradley Ogden at Lark Creek in California, Hastings was first exposed to the farm-to-table movement, which largely shaped his own vision and led him back to Alabama and what would eventually become a place in the Southern food movement.

Heading back south, the couple founded Hot and Hot Fish Club in 1995, and the rest is highly decorated

history. Named after a 19th Century epicurean club that Hastings's long-lost relative belonged to, Hot and Hot is steeped in Southern tradition—among the most important, the constant championing of Alabama farmers and fishermen. In fact, Chef Hastings is credited with being the first to bring the farm-to-table concept east of the Mississippi, with continued collaborative efforts involving local purveyors, foragers, and artisans. The menu changes daily, as seasonal ingredients become available, true to the rhythms of the countryside.

"Nature gives us nanoseconds within a season for ingredients like wild mushrooms, elderberries, honeysuckle, or wild strawberries. If you're not on everywhere, and I've made it my life's business to find it through food."

This very idea led us to Oregon last autumn, to saddle up horses, traverse the upland habitat of a sprawling 80,000-acre ranch to see if we couldn't take advantage of the seasonal bounty, and come up with dinners the old-fashioned way—through personal harvest. Our company included a cast of characters as rough as the surrounding rock bluffs, with a few seasoned cowboys to handle the horses, trainers to handle the dogs, and guides to handle, well, us. It's uncanny how quickly camaraderie and fellowship develop when you walk wild hills in pursuit of the same goals, with the same passions. This hunt was no exception.

> *"Nature gives us nanoseconds within a season for ingredients like wild mushrooms, elderberries, honeysuckle, or wild strawberries. If you're not on that one hill in eastern Alabama at just the right time, you're gonna miss it."*

that one hill in eastern Alabama at just the right time, you're gonna miss it. Understanding this cycle allows you to take what nature gives you, celebrate it, and move on," Chef Hastings said about their foraging efforts. This way of approaching food from nature's schedule, instead of their own, is just one of the factors that has brought Chris and Idie Hastings success at Hot and Hot Fish Club, and earned the restaurant the reputation as one of the best in the South (some might argue the country). Choosing early on to divide and conquer, the couple split duties, with Chris handling the culinary and public relations avenues, and Idie focusing on general management and front-of-house management. "The work Idie does with our staff, and managing me, is at the very heart of our success," he told me with a smile.

Over the past 20 years, their teamwork has garnered award after accolade, and culinary fame after good fortune. As if he wasn't already a household name in Alabama, Hastings in 2012 was presented the 2012 James Beard Award for Best Chef: South. "We want to celebrate where our boots are, and for the food to taste like right here. These types of opportunities are

Journeying from our rustic tent camp, we rode into the heart of upland country, trusting the experienced horses that have navigated the sheer, rocky terrain their entire lives. Often battling gale-force winds, we'd rein up to dismount whenever the English pointers caught a scent, so elegantly performing the task that breeding has developed through centuries.

Our objective was to put enough food on the table for 10 men. Strong winds, unfamiliar guns, and wily birds often leave an empty table, but we quickly found our shooting stride, and as the game bags began to fill, so did our hopes for dinner. Hastings downed birds with a practiced confidence that comes from a lifetime of seasonal pursuit in the field.

"I've been an outdoorsman my whole life. It's how I find solace from the twelve- to fourteen-hour days in the kitchen. In September I'm dove hunting, October I'm after upland birds and woodcock, December and January are all about the ducks, and of course in spring there's turkeys. The rest of the time, and in between, I fish," he says.

Thankfully, our quest concluded with enough daylight left to make it back to camp and build the centerpiece

Reindeer moss foraged
from the nearby Oregon
woods added yet another
wild ingredient.

of this experience—the cooking fire. As guns were broken down, horses unsaddled, and chukar removed from game bags, Chef Hastings quickly went to work prepping for what would become a fall feast—and a display of cooking the likes of which we had never seen and will likely never forget. The rough-wood table was swiftly transformed into a beautiful spread of seasonal ingredients, with found pinecones, thistles, and elk antler sheds complementing the whole birds yet to be plucked, and bottles of wine from Rob Mondavi set out to breathe.

As the chukar were prepped, livers and hearts set aside for an appetizer, Hastings continued to explain his life's passion in seeking opportunities such as these, which speak to the place you're in, in sync with the seasons. He talked of his love for open-fire cooking,

HORSEBACK HARVEST

The hunt proceeded atop horses, allowing them to cover more ground in search of wild birds.

which started when he was a boy, and how it would allow us to really taste the birds.

Leaving the cook fire to chase the quietly fleeting light, I noticed reindeer moss growing on the north sides of some trees. Having seen it used in dishes before, I thought I'd bring it back to Chef Hastings to gauge his interest. When Hastings saw me, he enthusiastically shouted, "Go get more!" I went back and filled my Stetson to the brim.

It was a wild moment, in a wild place, and one that not only added to the experience, but also brought full circle the philosophy that Chef Chris Hastings strives for in every meal. The ensuing hour and a half was the most impressive display of cooking I've ever seen, but not because of fancy ingredients or difficult techniques—quite the opposite. Here was a man in his element, at the pinnacle of his life's pursuit, confidently shaping nature's gifts into a meal with meaning, of both time and place, using only the most basic tool—fire. It was art in motion, a performance of passion, unclouded by restaurant tables or reservations or lofty ideals, in

**GRILLED
WHOLE CHUKAR**
Recipe on page 188

tune with the environment, the season, and the basic elements. It was one hell of a show.

As the birds were cooked whole in a cast iron skillet, Chef Hastings simultaneously prepared a fall salad, and a hunter's risotto made from Carolina gold rice—a heritage grain his ancestors grew—which was revived from history only 20 years ago. The cowboys stood in awe and silent observation of the creation of that meal, cooked completely over an open fire. From the use of hearts and livers, to frying the foraged moss in olive oil, it was something altogether foreign to them. You might say their first culinary rodeo, but one hopes not their last.

On our final day in Oregon, Hastings told me: "Everything about this trip was an homage to the period of my life when I knew where I was, what opportunities I was provided with, and how to use them. We cooked a simple meal, celebrated life in the moment, and ate food where our boots were."

Hastings's new restaurant OvenBird is a direct translation of the kind of cooking we experienced in Oregon. It is a live-fire-only restaurant, channeling the simple nature of cooking with flames. "Where Hot and Hot Fish Club has evolved into a very high-touch restaurant, OvenBird aims to be the opposite of that, with foods cooked entirely over fire, uncomplicated, intense in flavors, and presented as they are. We won't even have a gas line in the restaurant," Hastings told me. Employing the use of an asado, cauldrons, and a plancha, he says their mission is to "get back into life's rhythms one fire at a time."

Though cooking professionally doesn't always allow for rugged experiences in the restaurant, they come through in his intended, seasonal approach, which is a constant reminder of the bounty offered by nature, and the respect it deserves. Much as the Old Man taught the Boy in Ruark's classic novel, Chef Hastings, through his thoughtful process of preparing and cooking meals, is passing on a sort of culinary folklore—a historical record of time and place, and of Southern traditions.

**CHUKAR HEART AND
LIVER TOAST WITH
MUSCADINE JAM**
Recipe on page 43

FROM THE FIELD

Big & Small Game

PREExamPARING BIG GAME

Tips and techniques for the new hunter,

the do-it-yourself butcher, or the experienced sportsman

KEVIN GILLESPIE

What are your recommended steps to cleaning and butchering big game?

The number one concern is sanitation. You must ensure that the meat itself does not come in contact with any foreign substance. It's very hard to do with hair, bugs, and dirt all around. In a perfect world, my preference is to eviscerate the animal in the field, but carry it out intact and do the processing off-site, where you have clean tables and knives. I leave the internal organs in the field, providing a food source for other animals. If you cannot do that, then quarter the animal, eviscerate it, then break it down into smaller sections in order to carry it out. That means you cut it into four pieces. I prefer not using this method because it involves cutting through some of the best cuts.

My version: Make an incision up the belly just deep enough to get through the skin. Do that from the top of the genitalia to the base of the neck, being careful not to cut too deep and puncture the cavity. Use a very sharp, thin knife, and cut under the skin but above the meat to peel it back. Open it up like a book, along the line of the cut you just made, trying to remove excess skin and give yourself a clean shot

at the center section. Then make an incision that goes up each leg, like drawing a line from first cut up to the hooves of the animal; repeat the process of cutting under the skin, and getting room to work.

Continue the process of pulling the skin back, working around the entire animal. Try to cut the skin all the way down so the fur is touching the ground. The membrane separating the fur and the meat is uncontaminated since it already touched the meat, so you are making yourself a sort of tarp to work on.

Then go to the shoulders. Take a shoulder in hand and move it back and forth to see how the joint moves naturally. Make an incision beside the shoulder blade, which takes you to the joint. Cut through the ligaments and tendons, and take the shoulder off. Store in game bags. Some look like mesh or cheesecloth, and others are solid. The choice is based on the ambient temperature and how long you'll be using the bags. If you will be in the field for several days, use mesh so the meat breathes and does not rot. If you are packing out, or the meat will be in a refrigerator in the next several hours, use a solid bag to prevent blood and so on from getting

all over. Set the bag on a rock or hang it from a tree branch so it doesn't touch anything.

For the hind legs, do the same thing as for the shoulders to get a sense for how it's attached. Go in the side of the leg and make a 90-degree cut (up and down) and find the joint inside there against the bone at the bottom of the spinal cord. Use a knife to cut the connective tissues, removing the leg in one piece. It will be narrow at the bottom where the hoof is, and big and round at the top. It looks like a club or a ham. Then you're 90 percent done.

Be delicate with the backstrap (loin), the shoulders, and the sirloin (rear loin). These are the prime cuts you miss with quartering. Go just above the rib cage, using a knife to cut along the cage line. It's curved—follow the bone. Peel the back loin. Repeat on both sides. Bag and hang. If you want the tenderloin, you will have to eviscerate because it's inside the cavity. Make an incision in the clear open belly below the

rib cage. You'll see all the internal organs. Pull them out. Once all are removed, the tenderloin will be on the backside of where you cut off the loin. Remove just as you removed the loin, against the bone—it's easy to take out.

What type of equipment do you need when cleaning game?

I utilize separate cutting boards. All of mine are wood, but I note which ones I use for raw meat. They are not unsafe, but I use harsher cleaning chemicals on the ones I use for raw meat, and I don't want to do that to all of my cutting boards, so I keep them separate for that reason. Plastic or composite or wood is a matter of personal taste. Invest in a meat saw, which is like a hacksaw with a different blade for bone. You'll also need a small meat-cutting knife (7 or 8 inches long, in a scimitar shape, with a curved, stiff blade). You will use this to debone. A thinner-bladed slicing knife is best for removing silver skin and connective tissue without damaging the meat. A cleaver is good for cutting through joints; it's not necessary, but helpful. Don't forget disposable gloves. It's very important that everything is clean, from equipment to hands.

What types of seasonings are good for big game?
From a seasoning standpoint, venison is more akin to lamb than beef. Use the same pungent flavors that you use with lamb: chili peppers, rosemary, garlic, sage, thyme, and exotic spices such as curry powder and harissa. This meat can handle that profile. When I sculpt a dish around cuts of venison, I like to remember how lean it is. Either play it down—fresh, light, healthy (grilled, simple seasoning, served with other grilled vegetables and a light vinaigrette)—or play it up. Most people try to overpower the flavor. Good processing and butchering are very important to the flavor profile.

What is the secret for cooking something good and consistent?
The secret to cooking wild game is to understand the makeup of the meat. Wild game is extremely lean and does not have a lot of intramuscular fat. Every cut inside deer or elk is similar to beef tenderloin. The main rule is to avoid overcooking. Also remember that it's a wild animal, so it gets lots of exercise. Imagine the animal in five pieces: front shoulders, back legs, and center trunk.

The general rule is that the cuts in the center trunk are less exercised and more tender. Treat these like steak cuts: they are tender and require little cooking, so don't overcook. The other four sections get lots of exercise and fall into the brackets of stewing and slow roasting. They need time and opportunity for connective tissue to break down to tenderize. That's why people use cuts like front shoulders for stews, such as venison chili. Think of using these cuts as you would like a chuck roast. They make great medium-rare burgers. Don't overcook, or they will taste "livery," because overcooking amplifies the "gaminess," which is caused by higher levels of iron. Either cook these cuts very rapidly or very slowly. There really is no middle ground. Braising cooks up just like beef chuck or pot roast or stewing. The downside is

> *The secret to cooking wild game is to understand the makeup of the meat. Don't overcook, or they will taste "livery," because overcooking amplifies the "gaminess," which is caused by higher levels of iron. Either cook these cuts very rapidly or very slowly. There really is no middle ground.*

that you don't have the fat so you can still dry it out. I add some bacon or pork fat, to the braise and make sure the sauce has viscosity to coat the meat.

One cut that is an exception is the leg filet. This is difficult to obtain and requires advanced butchery. Using the rear legs, take the bone out, separate the muscles from one another following the natural seam, cut away the connective tissue, and you can cut steaks from that and they are really tender. It's worth the trouble! This is my favorite cut. All the trim becomes stew meat, like what you get out of the shoulder.

What is the best practice for freezing game?
Freezing big and small game is a really good idea. There's a lot of concern about parasites, even though I have never experienced these in my life and almost always eat the meat fresh. But freezing kills parasites and makes the meat safer. For freezing, the less oxygen, the better. Use a home vacuum device to help prevent freezer burn on the meat. Don't forget to label it! You think you will remember, but you won't. Pack for how you will use (four pieces at a time, and so on). Always put a date on the label. You'll have a shelf life of about a year. There is some flexibility to that date. If you went hunting early in the season and froze something in September, it should be fine into the next season, so you could eat it in November of the next year. It could deteriorate in quality but won't be unsafe. Just be sure you don't get the batches mixed up. ✌

Benton's Bacon-Wrapped Rabbit with Cabbage, Roasted Carrots, and Mustard-Glazed Turnips

CHEF JOSEPH LENN | SERVES 4

INGREDIENTS

1 whole rabbit (6 ounces rabbit leg meat)
2 ounces Benton's bacon
1 teaspoon salt
¼ teaspoon black pepper
½ head of cabbage

1. With a sharp knife, remove the hind legs and front legs from the rabbit. Next, carefully remove the loins, leaving the belly attached, and reserve it. Remove the meat from the back legs.

2. Season rabbit leg meat with salt. Place the leg meat and bacon into a grinder. Grind two times until the meat is thoroughly mixed. Place ground meat mixture into a piping bag and cut the tip of the bag, making a hole about the size of a dime.

3. Next, lay the reserved rabbit loin down flat on a cutting board and season both sides with salt and pepper. Using the prepared piping bag, squeeze ground meat in a tubular shape all the way down the loin. Roll the rabbit loin up, wrapping it snugly around the loin and ground meat stuffing.

4. Wrap sliced Benton's bacon around the rabbit loin. Using plastic wrap, roll up the stuffed rabbit loin into a tube shape, making sure the ends are tight and they stay covered. Reserve.

5. In a sauté pan, heat the canola oil until shimmering, using medium-high heat. Discarding the plastic wrap, place the prepared loin into the pan and sear until the bacon browns. Once seared nicely, place the loin in a 350-degree oven and cook until internal temperate is 140 degrees. Remove the loin from the pan, and let it rest.

6. Halve a cabbage, and shave it thin. Using the pan in which the rabbit was roasted, melt 1 teaspoon butter over medium heat. Add the cabbage and cook until wilted (3 to 4 minutes.)

FOR THE ROASTED CARROTS AND SHALLOTS

Olive oil
½ pound baby carrots
½ pound shallots, halved

1. Pour olive oil in a sauté pan over medium-high heat, heating this until it shimmers.

2. Place baby carrots and shallots in the pan and sear until brown (about 1 minute).

3. Transfer to a 350 degree oven, and cook carrots until tender (6 to 8 minutes.)

FOR THE MUSTARD-GLAZED TURNIPS

½ pound baby turnips (quartered)
½ cup Dijon mustard
¼ cup whole-grain mustard
¼ cup sorghum

1. Fill a large sauce pot with water, 2 inches from the top. Over high heat, bring water to a boil. Working in batches, blanch the turnips until tender (2 to 3 minutes).

2. Place turnips in a strainer to drain the excess water. Next, put the turnips in a sauté pan, then add Dijon mustard, whole-grain mustard, and sorghum. (The recipe makes more than you will need.)

3. Warm over medium heat, stirring the mixture to glaze the turnips (3 to 4 minutes). Reserve and keep warm.

To Serve: Slice the finished rabbit into disc shapes, about six slices per rabbit loin, season with salt, and divide onto four plates, placing three slices per plate over the prepared cabbage. Finish by dividing the carrots and turnips on the plate.

KEVIN GARRETT

Beer-Braised Buffalo Short Ribs

CHEF SEAN FINLEY | SERVES 4

INGREDIENTS

Four 3-bone portions of buffalo
  short ribs
2 bottles of Kentucky Bourbon
  Barrel Ale beer
1½ quarts beef broth
4 to 6 cloves fresh minced garlic
Kosher salt
Ground black pepper
4 to 6 sprigs fresh thyme
2 sprigs fresh rosemary
Mashed Potatoes (recipe
  following)
Honey-Roasted Carrots
  (recipe following)

1. In a deep roasting pan, add the beer, beef broth, minced garlic, salt, pepper, fresh thyme, and rosemary. The liquid level should be about two inches deep.

2. Sear the ribs on all sides in a hot skillet with a little olive oil, salt, and pepper. Arrange the ribs in the roasting pan; add additional beef stock if necessary to bring the level of the liquid just to the top of the ribs.

3. Cover the roasting pan tightly with two layers of aluminum foil and place in a 300 degree oven for six hours to braise.

4. Remove the pan from the oven and allow the ribs to rest warm. Use two cups of the braising liquid to make a gravy for the ribs by bringing the liquid up to a low boil in a small pot, re-season with salt and pepper to taste, and thicken with a cornstarch slurry.

FOR THE MASHED POTATOES

4 peeled, chopped russet potatoes
Whole milk
Unsalted butter
Kosher salt
White pepper

1. Boil the potatoes in water until they are tender enough to mash (usually 15 minutes in boiling water). If a knife blade pierces the potato with ease when you pick it up, and the potato slides off of the blade without effort, they are ready to mash.

2. Place the hot potatoes into a deep dish or bowl, adding butter, milk, salt, and white pepper.

3. Mash the potatoes with a potato masher until they are creamy but with small lumps remaining.

4. Season to taste with salt and pepper. Keep warm for serving with the ribs.

FOR THE HONEY-ROASTED CARROTS

1 pound baby carrots, cut in half
Kosher salt
Ground black pepper
Olive oil
Honey

Toss the carrots with olive oil, salt, and pepper. Place them on a roasting pan lined with parchment paper. Roast for 15 to 20 minutes at 400 degrees until the carrots are still crisp but browned. Remove from the oven and drizzle with honey. Keep warm until serving.

To Serve: Serve the ribs with the Mashed Potatoes and Honey-Roasted Carrots.

Chef's Note: When preparing the potatoes, let the "kitchen force" be with you—like your grandmother always did—to determine the amount of butter and milk to add. You will know as you mash.

Bacon-Wrapped Venison Tenderloin with Red Wine Gorgonzola Sauce

CHEF DOUG MACK | SERVES 4

Chef's Note: Venison has very little fat, so wrapping the filet with bacon keeps the meat juicy and imparts a nice smoky taste to the meat.

INGREDIENTS

4 venison tenderloin steaks (about 6 ounces each)
4 strips bacon
Red Wine Gorgonzola Sauce (recipe following)

1. Wrap each steak around its outside edge with a slice of bacon. Secure the bacon slices with toothpicks.

2. Grill or sauté the steaks much the same way as you would cook a beef tenderloin.

FOR THE RED WINE GORGONZOLA SAUCE

½ cup mushrooms
1 tablespoon oil
1 teaspoon flour
1 cup beef or venison stock
¼ pound Gorgonzola cheese
1 cup red wine
1 teaspoon basil

1. In a saucepan, simmer the mushrooms in the oil.

2. Add the flour and then the remaining ingredients. Simmer until smooth and thick.

To Serve: Ladle an equal pool of the Gorgonzola Sauce onto each plate, then place finished tenderloin on its center.

"We had always served game at our restaurant. But we wanted a seasonal event that centered on game and would introduce a sophisticated, adventuresome audience to new, out-of-the-ordinary foods. We wanted to reach beyond our usual venison burger and give guests the opportunity to try something they wouldn't usually eat. I see food as a venue for change, and feel it's important to connect to restaurants."

—CHEF DOUG MACK

Elk Vindaloo

CHEF KEVIN GILLESPIE | SERVES 4

INGREDIENTS

12 ounces boneless elk loin, cut into 1-inch pieces

½ cup malt vinegar

2-inch piece Ceylon cinnamon stick

2 tablespoons black peppercorns

1 tablespoon cumin seeds

1 tablespoon coriander seeds

1 tablespoon fennel seeds

3 tablespoons ancho or other ground chili powder

1 tablespoon red pepper flakes

1 teaspoon ground turmeric

¼ teaspoon ground cardamom

⅛ teaspoon ground cloves

1 jalapeño pepper, stem removed

3-inch piece fresh ginger, peeled and diced, about ⅓ cup

½ cup garlic cloves, peeled

3 shallots, diced, about ½ cup

½ cup grapeseed oil or canola oil

1½ cups chicken stock

1 medium Yukon Gold potato, peeled and cut into ½-inch dice, about 1 cup

2 teaspoons Kosher salt

1 lemon

1 tablespoon plus 1 teaspoon honey

½ cup plain Greek yogurt or other strained yogurt

½ cup fresh cilantro leaves, finely chopped, plus more for garnish

1. In a large bowl, toss the diced elk with the vinegar.

2. Break the cinnamon stick into pieces in a heavy skillet, then add the peppercorns, along with the cumin, coriander, and fennel seeds. Toast over medium heat until fragrant and deep golden brown, shaking the pan occasionally, about 4 minutes. The spices will start popping and dancing in the pan. Dry roast the spices a little longer than you might think is right; you want to develop some color on them, which adds more flavor. Once they start smoking, dump them from the skillet onto a piece of parchment or wax paper. Reserve the skillet.

3. When the spices have cooled a bit, grind them to a powder in a spice grinder or using a mortar and pestle. Transfer the ground spices to a bowl, and whisk in the chili powder, red pepper flakes, turmeric, cardamom, and cloves until well blended. Set this mixture aside.

4. In a food processor fitted with the metal blade, combine the jalapeño, ginger, garlic, and shallot, and process to a fine chop.

5. Return the reserved skillet to medium heat, and add the oil. When the oil is shimmering, add the chopped jalapeño-ginger mixture. Stir frequently, and if the mixture starts to brown, remove the pan from the heat to cool it a bit, then return to a lower heat setting; you want to slowly fry and brown the shallots without burning them. Scrape and stir the browned bits until the ingredients are evenly golden, 8 to 10 minutes. Add the ground spice blend, and cook for another 30 seconds. Stir in the elk and vinegar, stirring until the elk is completely coated with the spice mixture. Add the chicken stock, potatoes, and salt, and increase the heat to medium-high. Cover and bring to a boil, then decrease the heat to low, and simmer for 30 minutes.

6. After 30 minutes, remove the lid from the pot and simmer just until the sauce breaks or starts to separate, about 3 minutes. This will leave an oil slick on the top of the sauce. Remove the pan from the heat.

7. Squeeze the lemon into a small bowl to make a little more than ¼ cup lemon juice. Into this, whisk in the honey, yogurt, and cilantro.

Chef's Note: This is a pretty spicy dish. For less heat, remove the ribs and seeds from the jalapeño or just use a little less. Ceylon cinnamon sticks have a shaggy look similar to thin tree bark and are soft and crumbly, making them easy to grind. Look for them in Latin American markets or specialty food shops (Walmart stocks them too). If you can't find Ceylon cinnamon, substitute ¼ teaspoon ground cinnamon. But don't be tempted to use thick, hard cinnamon sticks (cassia); they won't grind easily.

Braised Elk Chuck Roast with Puttanesca Sauce

CHEF JOSH DRAGE | SERVES 8

INGREDIENTS

5 pounds elk roast (chuck roast)
Half bottle of red wine
2 medium onions
3 carrots
6 peppercorns
6 garlic cloves
2 bay leaves
6 fresh thyme sprigs
Veal stock—amount variable
Puttanesca Sauce (recipe following)
Roast Tomato Base (recipe following)
Crispy Eggplant (recipe following)

1. In a Dutch oven, brown the sides of the roast. When browned, remove the roast temporarily to a plate or board, and deglaze the roasting pan with the red wine. Add the roast back into the pot along with all other ingredients except for the stock.

2. Fill the Dutch oven about two-thirds of the way with veal stock. Cover, and cook the roast in the oven for up to 6 hours on a very low heat (250 degrees). Roll the roast over every so often to keep it moist, and check the level of liquid, readjusting as necessary by adding more stock so the pot does not dry out.

3. Uncover, and cook for another hour, first rolling the roast over in the pot again. The meat is done when it pulls apart easily, even if this is less than the stated six hours of cooking time.

4. Remove the elk from the cooking liquid to a platter or cutting board, and cool. Once cooled, tear the meat apart into about 3- to 4-ounce pieces, removing and discarding any unwanted parts.

5. Meanwhile, reduce the remaining cooking liquid from the roast until it becomes thick and rich. Add a portion of this to the Puttanesca Sauce, to meld all the flavors.

6. Lay the reserved elk in the finished Puttanesca Sauce in the sauté pan, warming this through.

FOR THE PUTTANESCA SAUCE

3 tablespoons oil
2 shallots, chopped
3 to 6 garlic cloves, minced
1 medium onion, chopped
12 anchovies
6 Roma tomatoes, finely chopped
1 cup Pinot Grigio
2 cups Roast Tomato Base (recipe following)
1 cup Kalamata olives
2 tablespoons capers, drained
2 roasted red peppers, chopped
1 teaspoon chili flakes
½ cup Italian parsley leaves, fresh
6 basil leaves, fresh
1 tablespoon marjoram, fresh
Reduced cooking liquid from the elk

1. Put the olive oil in a large, straight-sided saucepan and add the chopped shallots, garlic, and onion. Cook over high heat for a short time, just enough to soften the vegetables but not really brown them.

2. Stir in the anchovies, allowing them to melt, about 2 minutes.

3. Add the tomatoes to the pan and continue cooking for about a minute. Deglaze with white wine, and reduce by half.

4. Add in 2 cups of the Roast Tomato Base, olives, capers, roasted red peppers, and chili flakes. Simmer over a low heat for 30 minutes, add the cooking liquid from the elk, and turn off the heat. Stir in the fresh herbs, blending these in well, and reserve.

FOR THE ROAST TOMATO BASE

12 whole Roma tomatoes
1 head garlic
½ cup olive oil
Pinch salt
Pinch red chili flakes

1. Toss all the ingredients in a bowl, leaving the tomatoes whole. Add to a baking dish and roast at 400 degrees for about 30 to 45 minutes.

2. Remove from the oven and leave to cool, then run through a food mill to remove the skins, discarding these.

"My grandmother taught me to cook in Dutch ovens. They've always been popular on ranches because they can go into an oven or over a fire." —CHEF JOSH DRAGE

---

3. Use the prepared base in making the Puttanesca Sauce.

FOR THE
CRISPY EGGPLANT
2 eggs
2 cups milk
1 eggplant, sliced into ½-inch rounds
1 cup flour
4 cups panko breadcrumbs
Salt and pepper

1. Whisk the eggs and milk together in a medium-sized bowl.

Place the breadcrumbs and the flour separately into two other medium bowls, to prepare for breading. Dip each slice of eggplant first into the flour, then into the egg/milk mixture, then into the breadcrumbs, setting them aside to drain on a plate.

2. Once all of the eggplant is coated, brown these in a pan over medium heat, using a small amount of olive oil. This will provide a richer flavor to the finished dish, and will also cook

the eggplant all the way through and crisp the outside. When done, season with salt and pepper.

To Serve: Place the Crispy Eggplant on a serving plate and cover with some of the Puttanesca. Top with a serving of the Braised Elk in the sauce. Garnish with grated Parmigiano-Reggiano and fresh parsley, marjoram, or basil.

Paccheri Bolognese

CHEF GIANNI GALLUCCI | SERVES 4-6

INGREDIENTS

6 ounces ground beef
  (85 percent lean)
6 ounces ground veal
6 ounces ground pork
2 tablespoons extra-virgin olive oil
2 cloves garlic, finely chopped
3 bay leaves
Kosher salt, to taste
Freshly ground black pepper,
  to taste
2 medium white onions, finely
  chopped
2 celery stalks, finely chopped
2 carrots, peeled, finely chopped
½ cup dry red wine
3 cups of blended San Marzano
  tomato sauce
3 tablespoons tomato paste
1 pound paccheri pasta
Grana Padano cheese, for garnish

1. Heat oil in a large heavy pot over medium-high heat. Add chopped garlic. Let brown and add beef, veal, pork, bay leaves, and salt and pepper. Sauté, breaking up the meat and mixing as it cooks down, until browned. Drain all the fat from the pan.

2. Add onions, celery, and carrots, and sauté until soft, approximately 7 to 10 minutes. Add wine and boil for 1 minute. Add San Marzano tomato sauce, and reduce heat to very low. Cover sauce with lid slightly ajar and simmer over low heat for about 1½ hours, stirring occasionally.

3. Bring a large pot of water to a boil. Season with salt; add pasta and cook, stirring occasionally, until almost al dente. Drain. Reserve about a cup of pasta water.

4. Transfer sauce to a large skillet over medium-high heat. Add pasta and stir to mix pasta with the bolognese. Stir in some of the reserved pasta water if sauce seems dry.

To Serve: Divide pasta among warm plates. Top with fresh Grana Padano.

Hot and Hot Wild Venison Chili with Cilantro Crème Fraîche

CHEF CHRIS HASTINGS | SERVES 8

INGREDIENTS

2 pounds diced venison leg meat, cut into ½-inch cubes
3 thick slices bacon, chopped into ½-inch pieces
1½ cups yellow onion, diced
3 cloves minced, peeled garlic
1 cup black turtle beans, covered with 3 cups cold water and soaked in refrigerator overnight and drained
¼ cup dried chili mix
2½ tablespoons minced Anaheim chili peppers
1 cup canned tomato juice
½ teaspoon ground cumin seed
2 teaspoons chili powder
Pinch cayenne pepper
1 teaspoon Kosher salt
½ ounce unsweetened Hershey's chocolate
2 ham hocks
3 cups venison stock
1 tablespoon olive oil
1 cup tomato concasse, for serving
Cilantro Crème Fraîche (recipe following)

For the Cilantro Crème Fraîche

(yields one cup)
2 tablespoons chopped cilantro
2 tablespoons lime juice
1 cup crème fraîche

1. Combine all Cilantro Crème Fraîche ingredients in bowl until smooth. Reserve in refrigerator for serving.

2. Place a heavy-bottomed noncorrosive stock pot over medium-high heat. Add the bacon and cook, stirring often, until crisp and golden brown. Add the onion and sauté 1 minute, then add the garlic and sauté 30 seconds longer. Add the drained beans with the rest of the ingredients except the venison and tomato concasse. Reserve any remaining stock for later. Bring to a boil, reduce heat to a simmer and cook covered for 45 minutes.

3. Place a skillet over high heat and lightly coat the bottom with olive oil. Sear the meat quickly on all sides. Add the venison to the chili mixture and simmer uncovered for 1 hour or until the meat and beans are very tender. If necessary, add more stock during cooking. Taste and correct the seasonings. Remove the ham hocks, peel off the rind, remove the meat from the bones and add to the chili, discarding the bones.

To Serve: Serve the chili in heated bowls. Spoon 2 tablespoons of tomato concasse and a heaping tablespoon of Cilantro Crème Fraîche on each serving.

Chef's Note: Chili is almost always better the second day. If not using immediately, cool the pot in an ice bath and refrigerate. Reheat the cooled chili to simmer before serving.

Maple and Black Peppercorn Soaked Buffalo Tenderloin

CHEF DEAN FEARING | SERVES 4

INGREDIENTS

24-ounce whole buffalo tenderloin, trimmed of all fat and silver skin
1 cup maple syrup
2 tablespoons fresh cracked black pepper
2 cloves garlic, finely chopped
1 large shallot, finely chopped
1 teaspoon fresh sage, finely chopped
1 teaspoon fresh thyme, finely chopped
Crushed red pepper flakes, to taste
Salt and black pepper, to taste
2 tablespoons vegetable oil
Jalapeño Grits (recipe following)
Tangle of Greens (recipe following)
Yellow Tomato Pico de Gallo (recipe following)
4 sprigs fresh cilantro
Smoked chili aioli

1. In a small bowl, combine maple syrup, black pepper, garlic, shallot, sage, thyme, and pepper flakes. Stir to combine and add buffalo tenderloin. Let the meat marinate in the maple syrup mixture in the refrigerator for 8 hours or overnight, rotating the tenderloin every 2 hours. Remove tenderloin from the mixture and cut into 6-ounce steaks. Season with salt and pepper.

2. Heat oil in a large cast iron skillet over medium-high heat. When hot, lay buffalo in the skillet and brown for 4 minutes. Turn and brown for an additional 3 minutes or until desired degree of doneness is reached.

FOR THE JALAPEÑO GRITS

2 cups coarse white grits
1 tablespoon olive oil
4 ounces onion, diced
1 teaspoon minced garlic
1 tablespoon minced jalapeño
1 teaspoon fresh chopped thyme
6 cups chicken stock
1 teaspoon smoked paprika
½ ounce Tabasco

1. In a large saucepan (the grits will expand in volume during cooking), bring olive oil to medium-high heat.

2. Add onion, sauté for 2 minutes or until translucent. Add the garlic, jalapeño, and thyme. Add 6 cups of chicken stock, and bring to a boil.

3. Sprinkle in the grits a handful at a time, stirring constantly. Reduce heat to a simmer and cook the grits about 25 minutes, until they are thickened and soft in texture. Stir the grits occasionally as they cook.

4. Add smoked paprika and Tabasco, season with salt and pepper to taste.

FOR THE TANGLE OF GREENS

2 tablespoons olive oil
1 tablespoon shallots, minced
1 teaspoon garlic, minced
2 cups packed, washed stemless spinach
1 cup packed, washed arugula leaves
Salt and pepper

In a large sauté pan over medium-high heat, add the oil, shallots, and garlic. Sauté for 1 minute, add the greens, and continue to cook, stirring constantly. Continue to cook until the greens have wilted. Season with salt and pepper to taste.

FOR THE YELLOW TOMATO PICO DE GALLO

1 large yellow tomato, seeded and diced small
1 medium jalapeño, seeded and brunoise
1 small shallot, brunoise
1 lime, juiced
Salt and pepper

Combine ingredients in a small mixing bowl. Season with salt and pepper.

To Serve: Place jalapeño grits on the center of each plate. Cut each tenderloin on the bias through the middle and crisscross these on top of the grits. Place an evenly portioned tangle of greens and *pico de gallo* on each side of the tenderloin. On the front side of the tenderloin, spoon a pool of smoked chili aioli. Garnish with cilantro on top and serve.

Elk Loin with Celery Root and Pear Chutney

CHEF SCOTT OSTRANDER | SERVES 8

INGREDIENTS

3 pounds whole elk strip loin
2 pounds celery root bulb
2 pounds Idaho potatoes
½ cup whole milk
¼ pound whole butter
Salt and ground white pepper
3 pears, any type
¼ cup golden raisins
1 tablespoon minced red pepper
½ cup white wine vinegar
½ cup white sugar
½ cup water
1 tablespoon pickling spices

1. Peel celery root and potatoes. Cut into large dice and boil each separately, until tender.

2. Purée cooked celery root in a blender with the milk. Pass the cooked potato through a ricer or food mill. In a large bowl, fold together the potato, celery root, and butter. Season with salt and white pepper.

3. Peel the pears, remove the core, and cut into ¼-inch dice. Add the pears, raisins, red pepper, vinegar, sugar, and water to a saucepan and bring to a boil. Wrap all the pickling spices together in a coffee filter or cheesecloth, tie off with twine to make a bouquet garni, then add this to pot. Cook everything on medium heat until pears are tender and the liquid is close to dry. Remove the bouquet garni (which can now be discarded), and set aside the prepared pear chutney.

4. Season elk with salt and black pepper. Sear in a sauté pan on high heat until caramelized on each side, and then move to a 400-degree oven and roast to an internal temperature of 125 degrees. Allow to rest for 10 minutes, then carve into ¼-inch slices.

To Serve: Place the elk loin slices over the celery root and potatoes mixture and garnish with the pear chutney.

Slow-Smoked Beef Brisket

CHEF SEAN FINLEY | SERVES 4-6

Chef's Note: One of the main things to keep in mind when working with meat is to allow the meat to be at room temperature before any type of heat is applied to the meat for the cooking process. This prevents the fibers in the meat from "tensing up" by going from cold to hot too quickly, which will produce a tougher cut of meat.

INGREDIENTS

4 briskets
Beef Brisket Spice Rub (recipe following)
Coleslaw (recipe following)

For the Beef Brisket Spice Rub
(yields enough rub for one average size brisket)
¾ cup turbinado sugar
½ cup paprika
½ cup black pepper
½ cup garlic salt
¼ cup celery salt
¼ cup Kosher salt
3 teaspoons cumin
3 teaspoons ground coriander

1. Allow the briskets 2 to 3 hours at room temperature before putting them into the smoker.

2. Rub briskets down with spice rub and allow the seasonings to flavor the meat while they come up to temperature. The spice rub can be made ahead of time and stored in an airtight container.

3. Smoke at 200 degrees for 12 hours over hickory.

FOR THE COLESLAW

1½ heads green cabbage, chopped
½ head red cabbage, shredded
3 carrots, chopped
2 cups mayonnaise
½ cup sugar
1 tablespoon ground mustard
2 tablespoons ground black pepper
1 tablespoon celery salt
1 cup apple cider vinegar
Poblano pepper, diced

1. Mix all of the ingredients together in a mixing bowl using a wire whisk. Allow the flavors to marinate together. For a sweeter sauce, add sugar, a more tart sauce, add more vinegar.

2. Pour the coleslaw over chopped green cabbage, shredded red cabbage and carrots. Add in some fine diced poblano pepper for a "kick" to your slaw. Mix thoroughly with your hands and then chill the coleslaw until service.

To Serve: Slice the brisket across the grain of the meat for maximum tenderness. They each serve about four to five slices per guest, and always have more for seconds if requested.

Red-Wine Braised Venison Osso Buco with Six-Grain Risotto

CHEF SCOTT OSTRANDER | SERVES 8

INGREDIENTS

Eight 1-pound venison shanks
2 medium shallots, rough chop
4 garlic cloves
6 cups red wine (Cabernet, Syrah, or Shiraz)
4 sprigs fresh thyme
1 sprig fresh rosemary
12 cups chicken or beef stock
Cornstarch, as needed
2 cups prepared multigrain blend (mix of wild rice, farro, wheat berries, barley, quinoa)
2 tablespoons olive oil
4 tablespoons whole butter, divided
1 small yellow onion, minced
2 cups Arborio rice
1 cup white wine
½ cup grated Parmigiano-Reggiano cheese

1. Season shanks with salt and pepper. Add 2 tablespoons cooking oil to a large sauté pan, and sear on all sides until well caramelized, and then transfer to a deep baking dish.

2. Add the shallots and garlic to the hot pan, and cook until browned. Deglaze with the red wine and reduce by half.

3. Add the herbs and 6 cups of stock, and bring to a boil. Pour over the venison, and cover the pan with foil.

4. Cook in a 350-degree oven for 2 hours, 45 minutes.

5. Remove the venison from the pan and strain the liquid into a saucepan. Bring to a boil and reduce to one-quarter the original volume. Thicken with cornstarch as needed to reach the desired sauce consistency.

6. Cook the multigrain blend according to the package instructions. Set aside.

7. In a large saucepan, heat the olive oil and 2 tablespoons of butter. Add the onion and cook over low heat until soft and translucent. Add the Arborio rice and cook 2 to 3 minutes, stirring frequently.

8. Deglaze with the wine and cook dry. Add 2 cups of stock and bring to a simmer, stirring occasionally. When the pot is dry, add another 1 to 2 cups of stock. Continue the process until the rice is al dente. Fold in the multigrain mix, cheese, and remaining 2 tablespoons of butter.

To Serve: Transfer the rice to a large platter, and arrange the venison on the rice. Garnish with fresh herbs and serve with a side of the braising sauce and your favorite green vegetable.

Pork Shanks

CHEF HAL ROWLAND | SERVES 6

INGREDIENTS

6 pork shanks, each a 4-inch cut
Brine (recipe following)
1 gallon veal stock
1½ ounces garlic
7 ounces celery
1 onion
1 carrot
1 liter red wine
Glaze (recipe following)
Celery Root Purée (recipe
   following)

1. Brine the pork shanks for 24 hours. Remove pork from the brine, and drain; season with salt and pepper.

2. Sear the pork in oil in a rondeau (or brazier), reserving the oil when done.

3. To the oil, add the celery, garlic, onion, and carrots. Once everything is browned, add the red wine and reduce. Spoon the braise over the shanks, and cook in the rondeau at 275 degrees for 3½ hours, or until just tender.

FOR THE BRINE

½ cup salt
½ cup sugar
3 quarts sweet tea

Combine ingredients to create brine.

FOR THE GLAZE

(yields about 9 portions)
3½ ounces soy sauce
7 ounces sugar
4 ounces water

1. Place sugar and 1½ ounces water in a pan and bring to the consistency of caramel.

2. Deglaze with 2½ ounces of water and wait until it stops simmering. Add soy sauce and cool.

*FOR THE CELERY-
ROOT PURÉE*

(yields 14 ounces)
13 ounces peeled and diced
   celery root
10 ounces whole milk
Pinch Kosher salt

Combine all ingredients in pot and cook until tender. Purée in Vita-Prep or similar device until extremely smooth.

To Serve: Once the braised pork shank is fork-tender, place it in a pan with the glaze and spoon this over until the meat is lacquered. Serve the celery root purée beneath the sliced pork shank.

"I grew up in Waynesboro, Georgia, which is known as the bird-dog capital of the world. When I was a boy I used to put my shotgun across my handlebars and go bird hunting after school. The bird was almost always quail. And I've been bowhunting deer for 45 years. Long ago, I started grilling and making sausage to make the most of what I hunted."

—CHEF HAL ROWLAND

Tomahawk Ribeye Steak with Tomato Salad and Duck Fat Fries

CHEF KIPP BOURDEAU | SERVES 4

INGREDIENTS
1 ribeye steak (32 to 34 ounces)
Olive oil
Wine Salt (recipe following)
Sea salt, to taste
Coarse-ground pepper, to taste
Tomato Salad (recipe following)
Duck Fat Fries (recipe following)

1. Allow bone-in ribeye steak to come to room temperature, brush with olive oil, and season with sea salt and coarse-ground pepper.

2. Cook over medium heat and grill until desired readiness. Set aside to rest.

FOR THE WINE SALT
2 cups Cabernet wine
¼ cup coarse-ground sea salt
1 teaspoon sugar

1. In a medium-sized saucepan add wine. Reduce over medium heat until a syrup-like consistency is achieved and wine is reduced to about ¼ cup in volume. Remove from heat. Add sea salt and sugar and stir well. Let cool.

2. Place salt mixture on a baking sheet lined with a nonstick mat. Let mixture dry overnight in cool dry place. Place dried salt mixture in coffee grinder and pulse to a medium-coarse consistency. Set aside.

FOR THE TOMATO SALAD
1 pint heirloom cherry tomatoes, cut in half
1 red onion, sliced thin

2 cloves garlic, sliced thin
1 teaspoon white balsamic vinegar
1 tablespoon extra-virgin olive oil

In a medium bowl, add tomatoes, onion, garlic, vinegar, and olive oil, and toss. Season to taste with sea salt and pepper.

FOR THE DUCK FAT FRIES
4 cups clarified duck fat
2 Idaho potatoes, peeled and cut into 2- by ¼-inch cubes

1. In a large stockpot, add duck fat and bring to 275 degrees. Carefully add potatoes and blanch for 4 to 5 minutes. Remove potatoes from duck fat and place on a plate lined with a paper towel.

2. Increase temperature of fat to 350 degrees. Place potatoes back into duck fat and cook until golden brown.

3. Remove potatoes from oil and place on plate lined with paper towel, season with sea salt, and keep warm.

To Serve: Place ribeye steak in the center of a large cutting board. Arrange tomato salad next to the steak and fries on the opposite side. Sprinkle board with about 2 tablespoons of wine salt. Garnish with fresh herbs; serve immediately.

"Growing up on a gentleman's farm in Michigan, we grew and produced our own food because it was fun and natural. I appreciated the source of food in our fields and pens. I enjoyed bailing hay, feeding animals, and helping can our many vegetables. Spring always brings to mind the work of tapping maple trees, then transferring the sap to our around-the-clock outside stove, simmering twenty-four hours a day for two weeks. Homegrown/homemade has always been my mantra."

—CHEF KIPP BOURDEAU

Venison Short-Loin Filet with Tomato Basil Butter Sauce

CHEF TIM CREEHAN | SERVES 4

INGREDIENTS

Four 6-ounce venison short
loin filets (New Zealand
Red Stag)
½ cup of flour
2 tablespoons canola oil
½ cup chopped tomato
2 teaspoons chopped garlic
½ cup red wine
¼ cup More Than Gourmet
Classic French Demi-Glace
½ stick butter, chopped
2 tablespoons chopped fresh basil
1 recipe Sweet Potato Mash
(recipe following)
1 recipe Tobacco Onions (recipe
following)
Kosher salt, to taste
White pepper, to taste

1. Preheat oven to 400 degrees.
Season the steaks with salt and
pepper. Dust in flour. Heat the
oil in a sauté pan until almost
smoking. Add venison, and sear
on both sides. Place in the oven
for 10 to 12 minutes or to desired
doneness.

2. Remove the steaks from the
pan and keep warm. In the same
pan, add tomato and garlic; sauté
lightly. Add the wine and demi-
glace; cook until reduced by half.
Whisk in butter gradually until
fully incorporated. Stir in basil.

FOR THE SWEET POTATO MASH

1½ pounds sweet potatoes
½ stick butter
½ cup heavy cream
Salt, to taste
Black pepper, to taste

1. Peel and chop the potatoes.
Cover the potatoes with water in a
saucepan; cook until tender. Drain.

2. Remove to a mixing bowl.
Add butter, cream, salt, and
pepper; beat until smooth.

FOR THE TOBACCO ONIONS

1 medium onion
4 cups canola oil

1. Cut the onion into very thin
slices and separate into rings.
Preheat the oil to 350 degrees
in a large saucepan.

2. Add the onion rings to the hot
oil; fry for 20 seconds or until dark
brown. Place on a cloth or paper
towel to drain till crisp.

To Serve: Place filets on Sweet
Potato Mash, and top with
Tobacco Onions.

"This recipe is my signature
preparation of venison and
is offered year-round on the
Cuvee 30A menu; however, we
also find success with quail,
duck, and wild boar dishes.
We like to stuff or grill quail,
while duck and wild boar are
best slow-cooked to maximize
flavor and achieve tenderness.
Overcooking and dryness
tend to be the typical failures
in preparing game, detracting
from the appreciation of these
items at their natural best."

—CHEF TIM CREEHAN

Ground Venison Kabobs with Tomato Jam

CHEF KEVIN GILLESPIE | SERVES 4

INGREDIENTS

2 pounds venison, ground, 90% lean

2 tablespoons ice-cold water

2 cups fresh flat-leaf parsley, finely chopped

1 cup fresh mint, finely chopped

½ cup fresh cilantro, finely chopped

½ cup onion, finely minced

2 tablespoons za'atar

1 tablespoon plus 1 teaspoon salt

2 teaspoons garlic, finely minced

About 2 tablespoons grapeseed oil

About ½ cup Tomato Jam (recipe following)

1. Heat a grill for direct high heat.

2. In a large bowl, crumble the venison, and pour the ice water over the top. With gloved hands, gently mix in the parsley, mint, cilantro, onion, za'atar, salt, and garlic to combine. Divide into 4-ounce portions (about 10) and shape each into a log around a long metal skewer, pressing gently.

3. Scrape the grill clean, and coat it with oil. Brush the skewers all over with the oil, and grill for 2 minutes. Turn and grill for another 2 minutes, then turn one final time, and grill for 2 minutes more. The 6-minute cooking time is for medium-rare kabobs—the perfect doneness to serve venison. Transfer the kabobs to a platter and let rest for 5 minutes before serving.

FOR THE TOMATO JAM

(yields about 2 cups)

28-ounce can whole peeled plum tomatoes, with juice

6-ounce can tomato paste

½ cup onion, finely minced

½ cup dark brown sugar, packed

¼ cup red wine vinegar

3 tablespoons garlic, minced

1 teaspoon salt

¼ teaspoon ground cinnamon

1. Empty the can of tomatoes and juice into a heavy-duty, nonreactive, 3-quart saucepan.

2. Using your hands, squeeze and crush the tomatoes. Stir in the tomato paste, onion, sugar, vinegar, garlic, salt, and cinnamon, and bring the mixture to a boil over medium-high heat.

3. Reduce heat to medium-low, and simmer until the mixture thickens, stirring occasionally, about 45 minutes.

4. Remove from the heat and use an immersion blender or stand mixer to purée the mixture until smooth.

5. Return to heat, and simmer until it has a thick, jamlike consistency, another 10 minutes. Store, covered, in the refrigerator for up to 3 months.

To Serve: For each plate, spread a generous spoonful of tomato jam on the plate, and top with two kabobs.

Wild Boar Chops with Braised North Carolina Greens and Cranberries

CHEF SCOTT OSTRANDER | SERVES 8

INGREDIENTS

Sixteen 4-ounce wild boar
  rack chops
2 quarts Apple Cider Brine (recipe
  following)
4 pounds braising greens (kale,
  collards, chard, turnip, or
  mustard)
1 tablespoon cooking oil
1 cup dried cranberries
½ cup red wine vinegar
½ cup white wine
1 cup chicken or vegetable stock
2 tablespoons brown sugar
Salt and pepper, to taste

1. Prepare the chops, and place in the Apple Cider Brine for four hours or overnight.

2. Remove the chops from the brine, and pat dry.

3. To prepare the greens, rinse thoroughly in cold water to remove any sand, and roughly chop. Add the cooking oil to a large saucepan, add the greens, and sauté briefly. Add the vinegar, wine, sugar, and cranberries and cook. Cover on low heat, until the greens are tender. Season to taste with salt and pepper.

4. Heat grill to medium. Season the chops with salt and pepper, and grill for 5 minutes on each side, or to desired doneness.

FOR THE APPLE CIDER BRINE

2 cups water
⅓ cup Kosher salt
6 dry juniper berries
3 garlic cloves
1 bay leaf
3 fresh thyme sprigs
1 quart fresh apple cider
1 quart ice

1. Add the water, salt, spices, and herbs to a saucepan and bring just to a boil.

2. Transfer to a one-gallon container and add the cider and ice. Mix to combine.

To Serve: Place the boar chops over the greens, and garnish with additional cranberries.

"We brine our wild boar in a solution that's half salt brine, half apple cider. I like to serve the chops with house-made boar sausage, braised greens, and cranberries, for a variety of flavors and textures." —**CHEF SCOTT OSTRANDER**

Vermont Rabbit Cooked in Hard Cider with Apples

CHEF DOUG MACK | SERVES 4

INGREDIENTS

1 rabbit (3 pounds), cut into sections and the carcass removed for the stock
1 cup flour
1 teaspoon salt
1 teaspoon pepper
1 teaspoon paprika
3 tablespoons olive oil
2 Granny Smith apples, cut into wedges
Stock (recipe following)
2 cups hard cider
½ cup heavy cream or crème fraîche
1 tablespoon tomato paste

1. In a shallow bowl, combine the flour, salt, pepper, and paprika. Coat the rabbit pieces in the flour mixture, shaking off any extra. Set aside.

2. In a large frying pan, heat the oil over medium heat until hot but not smoking. Add the rabbit pieces and cook 3 minutes. Turn and cook until browned, 3 minutes more. Add the apples and sauté briefly. Add the stock and hard cider. Simmer for 30 minutes.

3. Add the cream and tomato paste, simmer 15 minutes, being careful not to bring the mixture to a boil.

FOR THE STOCK

4 quarts water
1 celery stick, coarsely chopped
1 carrot, coarsely chopped
1 medium onion, cut into quarters
Trimmed rabbit bones (reserved)

1. In a medium stockpot, simmer the water, celery, carrot, onion, and the rabbit bones. Bring the mixture to a boil and allow it to simmer until the mixture has reduced to a quart, which will take about 1½ hours.

2. Strain the stock, and reserve.

To Serve: Place the rabbit on a platter with the apples, spoon the sauce over it, and serve.

Chef's Note: The stock can be made ahead of time, so you have this as a base while you prepare everything else.

Grilled Whitetail Filet ❯

CHEF KEVIN GILLESPIE | SERVES 4

INGREDIENTS

1 pound venison filet (either leg
   or backstrap will work)
2 tablespoons rosemary,
   coarsely chopped
2 tablespoons garlic cloves, sliced
¼ cup Espelette pepper
½ cup extra-virgin olive oil
Kosher salt, to taste
Lime wedges, for garnish

1. Mix the rosemary, garlic, Espelette pepper, and oil together. Pour over the venison filet and place in a Ziploc storage bag. Allow the meat to marinate for up to 36 hours.

2. Remove from marinade and wipe excess marinade from the meat. Grill over high heat until medium rare. Serve sliced, with lime wedges as garnish.

Lamb Osso Buco

CHEF TIM CREEHAN | SERVES 8

INGREDIENTS

8 lamb shanks, about one and
   a half pounds
¼ cup thyme, chopped
¼ cup garlic, clove
2 cups Italian plum tomatoes,
   crushed
1 potato, diced
2 carrots, diced
1 yellow onion, diced
2 zucchinis, diced
2 yellow squash, diced
2 cups red wine
2 cups veal stock
Salt, to taste
White pepper, to taste

1. Preheat oven to 450 degrees. Season the lamb shanks to taste with salt and white pepper. Place the shanks in a roasting pan.

2. Add the thyme, garlic, tomato, potato, and vegetables. Cook for 45 minutes or until the meat and vegetables are brown. Add 1 cup of the red wine and cover the roasting pan with aluminum foil.

3. Cook for an additional hour or until the meat easily pulls away from the bones.

4. Place the roasting pan on a high fire, remove the foil, and add the remaining red wine and veal stock.

5. Reduce the stock to the desired consistency. Season to taste with salt and white pepper.

To Serve: Serve the lamb shanks topped with the vegetables and reduced sauce.

"In my time spent with friends, and in the questions that time nurtured about why and how I hunt, I found that my motivations revolve around something far deeper than the bits of flesh and feather I occasionally collect. What I seek in my hunting, and frankly what I don't always find, is that luminous quality that I believe Lewis and Clark recognized far better. In my hunting I've come to celebrate a place of mild discomfort that means I'm working for something, earning something, going just beyond what's comfortable for the privilege of killing something I cherish.

It's an ethos that has explained to me what it means to be a hunter and a human, and a philosophy that justifies the sore legs and the cold fingertips, and even the little bits of flesh and blood that I donate to the land I intend to take from. There is an equity there, something given for something gained, and just enough required of the human spirit to make it both resonant and worthwhile. This is no doubt a concept that Lewis and Clark and their Corps of Discovery understood, as they leaned into the discomfort and the periodic unknown, full of faith that in the journey there was value."

—REID BRYANT
"Discovering the Spirit"
June-July 2018, *Covey Rise*

BRIAN GROSSENBACHER

Rabbit Soup
CHEF ROB MCDANIEL | SERVES 6

"Rabbit hunting isn't something that I've done very often, but I have always been interested in the sport. Growing up, I knew a few rabbit hunters, and tagged along a few times. I think I enjoyed watching dog owners converse about the dog race the most. The ability of a dog's master to tell exactly what their dogs were doing just by the pitch in their bark or voice is pretty amazing to me. As we all know, rabbits are pretty fast, so hitting one can be a challenge, but I did catch on pretty quickly to a flaw that most rabbits have: They run in circles. So if you miss, you just wait, until they come back around again." **—CHEF ROB MCDANIEL**

INGREDIENTS

2 rabbits, whole
⅛ cup plus 2 tablespoons peanut oil
1 gallon chicken stock or water
2 sprigs of thyme
3 bay leaves
6 cloves garlic, minced
2 carrots, finely diced
1 large sweet onion, finely diced
2 ribs celery, finely diced
1 cup chopped kale, washed well and packed
Salt and pepper, to taste

1. Remove the front legs, the back legs at the joint, then quarter the remaining saddle.

2. In a large Dutch oven, heat ⅛ cup peanut oil over medium-high heat. In a large bowl, toss the rabbit with 2 tablespoons oil, salt, and pepper.

3. Just as the oil begins to smoke, lower the heat to medium and add half the seasoned rabbit. Brown on all sides, then remove and repeat with the remaining rabbit.

4. Once all the rabbit has been browned, pour off the grease then add rabbit back to the Dutch oven, along with 1 gallon chicken stock, thyme, bay leaves, and garlic. Bring to a low simmer and allow to cook, covered, for 45 minutes.

5. Remove rabbit and thyme, discard the thyme, and allow the rabbit to cool enough to handle. While the rabbit is cooling, add the carrots, onion, and celery to the simmering stock, and cook until carrots are tender, about 15 minutes.

6. Remove all meat from the bone, shred the meat, and then return it to the Dutch oven. Once the rabbit has been added, turn off the heat, and stir in the kale. Adjust the seasoning to your liking.

To Serve: Allow the soup to sit for 10 minutes before serving. Finish with a good drizzle of nice peppery extra-virgin olive oil, and serve with some crusty bread.

Venison Medallions with Mushroom Risotto and Sweet-Pepper Coulis

CHEF KIPP BOURDEAU | SERVES 4

FOR THE VENISON

1 pound venison tenderloin, trimmed, cut into medallions
1 tablespoon A.1. Steak Sauce
1 tablespoon soy sauce
2 tablespoon red wine
4 juniper berries, crushed
1 tablespoon coarse-ground pepper
1 tablespoon olive oil
Sprig of fresh rosemary

1. In large Ziploc bag, add steak sauce, soy sauce, red wine, juniper berries, pepper, olive oil, and rosemary. Mix well, place venison medallions in bag, and let marinate for 1 hour.

2. Remove venison from the marinade and pat dry with a paper towel. In a large sauté pan over high heat, add 1 tablespoon of olive oil. Place venison in the sauté pan and cook for about 3 minutes on each side until medium rare.

FOR THE RISOTTO

2 tablespoons unsalted butter
2 tablespoons minced shallots
1 cup Arborio rice
½ cup white wine
2½ cups chicken stock
2 cups crimini mushrooms, sliced
¼ cup fresh grated Parmesan cheese

1. In a medium saucepan over low heat, bring chicken stock to a low simmer. Meanwhile, add butter, shallots, and Arborio rice to a large sauté pan over medium heat, and sweat for 3 to 5 minutes. Add white wine to rice, and cook for 3 more minutes.

2. Add a third of the hot chicken stock, to the rice, and stir until rice the absorbs the stock; repeat until all stock is used and rice is almost fully cooked. In a medium sauté pan, cook mushrooms in a little olive oil or butter. Fold mushrooms and Parmesan cheese into cooked risotto.

FOR THE SWEET PEPPER COULIS

2 red peppers, roasted, peeled, seeds removed
½ cup chicken stock
1 tablespoon cornstarch dissolved with 2 tablespoons of chicken stock

1. In a medium saucepan over medium heat, add roasted peppers and chicken stock. Simmer for 5 minutes, then add cornstarch and simmer for 5 more minutes.

2. Purée in a blender until smooth. Keep warm.

To Serve: On four warm serving plates, divide the risotto evenly and place on center of each plate. Place three medallions of venison on each plate, drizzle with pepper coulis, garnish with herbs and onion sprouts; serve immediately.

SPORTING SKILL

Story by Miles DeMott | Photography by Terry Allen

Personally bringing game to the table and cooking deliberately, Scott Leysath lives the life of The Sporting Chef.

My first impression of Chef Scott Leysath came at the small baggage claim area of the Aberdeen Airport. Pheasant hunting is a $200 million industry in South Dakota, and Aberdeen is a busy port of entry for hunters—with their dogs—eager to claim their rental trucks, or to meet their guides and get on with it. The latest in sporting cases filled with the appropriate guns and wardrobe is standard travel gear, and Leysath carried those bags, too. But the most treasured of his accoutrements was an item found more typically in the arms of departing hunters: He was carrying a cooler.

Known as The Sporting Chef, Leysath has traveled the world with a gun in one hand and a carving knife in the other. His culinary ascension has been remarkable. His early work managing and owning restaurants affirmed his love of cooking and, at the same time, cast a light on a forested trail that only he could see, a path around the daily grind of food service that hung like an albatross around his culinary inclinations. He became more active in conservation groups such as Ducks Unlimited and California

Waterfowl, offering his cooking, writing, and editing expertise to their magazines. Those connections led to more cooking demonstrations at outdoor shows and hunting events that, in turn, led to more writing gigs with such magazines as *Wildfowl, Wetlands,* and *Cooking Wild.*

Next thing you know, Scott Leysath is an authority on cooking wild game. He made his television debut with HGTV's *Paul James' Home Grown Cooking,* and his popularity and authority opened doors on outdoor channels reaching across the country. Leysath answered with his award-winning show, *The Sporting Chef* on Sportsman Channel, which brought his particular talents to my attention. Quietly confident and unassuming, Leysath's anti-chef demeanor was the perfect complement to our common destination, a small lodge called Ringneck Retreat in Hitchcock, the heart of South Dakota pheasant country. But before we get there, let me tell you about the hunting and the conversation. Which brings me back to the cooler.

Leysath's cooler was no ordinary vessel. It was no pristine, sponsor-gifted Yeti with all the trimmings that caught my eye in the Aberdeen baggage claim area. Instead, Leysath hugged a nondescript Igloo cooler of an early vintage, secured by desperate handles and road-weary duct tape, with traces of

DUCK STIR FRY
Recipe on page 141

leafy vegetables springing defiantly from under the lid. My first thought was that somebody ought to get this guy a new cooler. By the end of the trip, I considered the old cooler his greatest badge of honor.

While it may be possible to become an expert on cooking wild game without ever picking up a gun, that's not the road Leysath took. From his early years in the woods of Northern Virginia to his more recent residency in the heart of California duck country, The Sporting Chef has always explored the most direct connection between field and fork. It was no surprise, then, to learn firsthand that Leysath was a good shot. Our hunt was obviously not his first. But the ability to bag pheasant was not his most significant performance afield. On the second day of hunting, I discovered the secrets of the ancient cooler and their connection to Leysath's greatest strength. While

unseasonably temperate, the December weather in South Dakota still had a bite—and a bite was what we needed after a chilly morning hunt. Returning to our trucks for a midday respite, we were treated to a fresh pheasant stew that brought many bowls back for seconds—and, dare I say it, thirds. The assemblage of pheasant, sausage, and assorted vegetables was prepared to perfection atop his Camp Chef stove in the middle of nowhere. It was, quite possibly, the finest meal afield I've ever experienced. It was wild game, prepared simply, and served appropriately. Hallmarks of The Sporting Chef.

The evenings at the lodge in South Dakota brought ample opportunity to wax philosophically over a good bourbon, and some famous chefs would welcome such an opportunity to explore *ad nauseam*

the ounce-by-ounce play-by-play of their most creative or innovative recipes; or the times they served the rich and famous at table. Knowing I was writing a story about him certainly afforded Leysath the opportunity to recite the litany of print outlets that came before me, or the many awards that feather his cap. It was an approach that he declined out of hand. Instead, we talked about life, liberty, and the pursuit of happiness, from a uniquely culinary perspective.

I asked Leysath, for example, what he would do if the world offered a blank slate. He sipped and thought and responded that he wouldn't really change anything. This life he'd evolved into was more than amply satisfying and, at times, even beyond his wildest imagination. His work required him to spend time afield and time in the kitchen, and these two passions melded together to provide a living wage and a compelling life story.

The culinary arts in today's media world are too often portrayed as the frenzied hyperbole of staged reality challenges and puff pastry wars. But that's not Scott Leysath, whose relaxed calm is at once refreshing and comfortable. The Sporting Chef is no stranger to camera and set, but his many years of corporate and event cooking have seasoned his people skills to absolute perfection.

If you're hunting a recipe for success, Thoreau suggested going in the direction of your dreams and living the life you imagine. Adapting Thoreau, it seems, Scott Leysath packs a few of life's spices into a vintage Igloo cooler, shoulders a trusty shotgun, and goes to the woods to cook deliberately.

FROM THE FIELD

Gamebirds & Fowl

PREPARING GAMEBIRDS

Tips and techniques for the new hunter,

the do-it-yourself butcher, or the experienced sportsman

CHRIS HASTINGS

How do you clean, skin, and pluck birds? What are some tips you recommend using?

There are two ways to go about cleaning gamebirds. My personal choice is to pluck the whole bird, keeping the skin on and intact, removing the viscera and the head and feet, washing the cavity, and drying it for a variety of stuffing options. When plucking the feathers, carefully pull them in the opposite direction from the way they lie down on the bird. There will be less tearing of the skin. The second option is to simply peel back the skin and feathers from the bird, exposing the breast meat, and bone out the breast.

Do you keep the skin on when preparing to eat the bird?

When possible, I really prefer gamebirds with the skin on. The skin brings fat, texture, and flavor that is very important for the best outcome of gamebird cooking.

What do you recommend to hunters on being creative on how they cook gamebirds?

The biggest opportunity to get creative with your gamebird recipes is with your sauces, vegetables, and starch arrangements. Here's why: I almost never change the way I cook the meat. It is perfect, and you risk detracting from the flavor with rubs, marinades, dressings, and so on.

What parts of the birds are edible and how should they be used?

Many parts of gamebirds are edible. Of course, I use the breast meat and the legs, but as a rule I always try to use the hearts and livers from gamebirds as well. They are very easy to cook, and delicious.

What is the best practice for breasting a bird?

I prefer plucking the bird and deboning with the skin on and intact. This adds flavor, texture, and fat.

What is the best practice when deboning a bird? Are there certain bones you keep in to help with cooking?

One of the questions I get a lot is: Do I cook birds bone in or boneless? As a rule, I prefer cooking anything with the bone in because of the flavor the bone brings to the party. That being said, it is either all on or all off. I rarely leave in small sections of bones.

What type of utensils, knives, etc do you need when cleaning a gamebird?

All you need to clean birds are a pair of poultry shears, a long paring knife with some flexibility, and a cutting board.

How long does meat last if frozen? Does the amount of freezer time matter?

As a rule, I do not carry over any game from season to season. So, I would recommend freezing only for a year at most.

How do you prepare it to be frozen? Is it different than normal?

The single best way to freeze game is by using a vacuum sealer. No air equals no freezer burn. Also, when thawing out your game, place in the fridge overnight in a bowl or dish. When it's thawed, remove from the bag, wrap the game meat in clean towels, and place on a platter in the fridge until ready to use.

How much time do you have in certain conditions, from the kill to icebox, and eventually preparation and eating?

I try to get game into the fridge whole, no more than eight hours after it's shot. One exception is wild turkeys. I hang whole wild turkeys at room temperature for two days, then clean and freeze them with no problems.

Are gamebirds prepared differently from each other? What tips do you have for the hunter who is cooking his own game?

Four tips that work for all gamebirds: First, marinate only in olive oil, fresh thyme, savory, sage, salt and pepper. Why? This does not step on the natural flavor of the meat the way rubs and marinades do. Second, bring the meat to room temperature before cooking. Third, do not overcook. Trust me, less is always more. Last, cook over wood and natural charcoal when you can. I use both together for the best results. Also, a hotter fire is better than a cooler fire.

Could you speak to honoring the bird and respecting the harvest? How and why do you honor the bird?

There is a dilemma we all face from time to time. We struggle with what to do with our harvest and the importance of our responsibility to honor the life we take. By this I mean to see that our harvest is eaten and not thrown away. As a young chef I was taught never to waste anything. I encourage people to never waste when harvesting any type of game.

Gamebird Posole Soup

CHEF CHARLIE PALMER | SERVES 6

Chef's Note: This dish falls into the heartwarming comfort food category. It's a great dish to make outdoors at the campsite, but certainly can be made in its entirety in advance and simply reheated.

INGREDIENTS

2 pounds boneless gamebird meat, cut into ½-inch cubes
3 tablespoons canola oil
1 chipotle pepper (from a can of chipotle peppers in adobo sauce), chopped
1 tablespoon adobo sauce (from the can of chipotle peppers)
Two 14½-ounce cans white hominy, drained and rinsed
One 14½-ounce can chopped tomatoes, with their juices
5 cups chicken stock
¼ cup fresh lime juice
½ cup chopped fresh cilantro
1 cup chopped scallions (about 6 scallions)
1 large jalapeño pepper, stemmed and thinly sliced
6 ounces queso fresco or Cotija cheese, crumbled
2 avocados, sliced
12 small radishes, quartered
12 warmed flour tortillas
Hot sauce, as condiment
Vegetable Mix (recipe following)
Spice Mix (recipe following)

For the Vegetable Mix

1 large yellow onion, chopped (about 3 cups)
1 large green bell pepper, cored, seeded, and chopped (about 1 cup)
1 large sweet red pepper, cored, seeded, and chopped (about 1 cup)

2 cups chopped green cabbage
8 garlic cloves, coarsely chopped

For the Spice Mix

1 tablespoon ground cumin
¼ teaspoon ground cinnamon
1 teaspoon ground coriander
1 teaspoon dried Mexican oregano
¼ teaspoon freshly ground black pepper
1 tablespoon Kosher salt

TO PREPARE

1. In a 6-quart stockpot, heat the canola oil over medium heat, add the gamebird meat, and cook until just lightly seared, 2 to 3 minutes.

2. Add the vegetable mix, and cook, stirring occasionally, until all of the vegetables are softened but have not yet begun to color, 5 to 7 minutes. Add the spice mix, chipotle pepper, and adobo sauce. Increase the heat to high, and cook, stirring, for 1 minute to get everything going.

3. Add the hominy, tomatoes, chicken stock, and lime juice, and bring to a boil. Lower the heat and simmer, covered, until the meat is tender, about 30 minutes.

To Serve: Ladle the soup into individual bowls, and garnish with the cilantro, scallions, jalapeño pepper, cheese, avocados, and radishes. Serve with warm tortillas and hot sauce.

"From a wild-game standpoint, so many people tell me recipes that are pretty crude. Game meat is lean, in general, so you have to introduce moisture by brining it or marinating it to give the meat a better chance of keeping moist, or use slow-braising to make ragouts, stews, and chilies. It's tasty meat to begin with, so you want to bring that flavor out without trying to cover it up. Too many people think of wild game and think of strong sauces or glazes that will cover up the taste of the game, as opposed to enhancing it and making it better."

—CHEF CHARLIE PALMER

Sous-Vide Quail

CHEF LESLIE SHEPHERD | SERVES 2-4

"This recipe was developed while searching for different ways to cook game. I cook quail frequently, almost daily, at the plantation. The sous-vide method has become a foolproof way of obtaining a moist and tender bird." —**CHEF LESLIE SHEPHERD**

INGREDIENTS

4 quail, spatchcocked
Salt and pepper, to taste
1½ tablespoons lemon juice,
    or to taste
6 teaspoons butter
¼ teaspoon Worcestershire sauce,
    or to taste
4 tablespoons canola oil

1. Preheat sous-vide water bath to 132 degrees.

2. Season birds well with salt and pepper. Place birds together in large bag, and sprinkle with lemon juice and Worcestershire sauce, then place a pat of butter on each bird. Vacuum pack the quail in a single layer.

3. When water reaches desired temperature, lower the bagged quail into the water bath, making sure it stays fully submerged, and cook for 1½ hours.

4. When the quail are ready, remove the bag from the water, and transfer them to a plate. Discard the liquid in the bag.

5. Pat the skin side of each quail dry with a paper towel or clean lint-free dish towel, then rub each bird all over with 1 tablespoon of oil.

6. Preheat a cast iron pan over medium-high heat. Place the quail, skin side down, on the pan, and cook until the skin has crisped and deeply browned to almost blackened, for 2 to 3 minutes. Using tongs, flip the quail over, and cook for 1 minute more.

To Serve: Combine more butter, lemon juice, Worcestershire sauce, salt, and pepper and heat over medium heat. Serve alongside quail for dipping.

Bacon-Wrapped Quail with Pickled Jalapeño Stuffing

CHEF BEN FORD | SERVES 8 AS A MAIN COURSE OR 16 AS AN APPETIZER

INGREDIENTS

16 semi-boneless quail (about
    4 ounces each), rinsed and
    patted dry
4 smoked ham hocks
2 tablespoons olive oil
½ cup minced shallots (about
    3 shallots)
8 garlic cloves, halved
¼ cup fresh thyme leaves
4 fresh dates (preferably Medjool),
    pitted and finely chopped
    (about ¼ cup)
3 pickled jalapeños, thinly sliced
32 slices bacon (about 1 pound;
    not thick-sliced, 4 to 5 inches)
16 fresh rosemary sprigs (about
    4 inches long)
Kosher salt and freshly ground
    black pepper

1. Cut the meat from the ham hock. Discard the skin and bones and finely chop the meat.

2. Heat the olive oil in a medium size sauté pan over medium heat. Add the shallots and cook them for about 2 minutes, until tender and translucent. Add the garlic and thyme, and sauté for another minute, stirring so the garlic doesn't brown. Add the ham hock meat, dates, and jalapeños and stir to combine.

3. Fill the cavity of each quail with 2 tablespoons of the stuffing. Place one rosemary sprig inside each quail.

4. Lay two slices of bacon in a T shape on your work surface. Lay the quail, breast up, on the bacon, centering it where the slices intersect. Bring each slice up and over, so that one wraps horizontally and the other vertically, and they overlap in the center. Continue stuffing and wrapping the remaining quail in the same way.

5. Place the quail breast side up on a baking sheet. Leave some space between the quail on the baking sheet. You may need to use two sheets.

6. Season the quail all over with salt and pepper. The quail can be prepared to this point a day in advance. Cover and refrigerate until you're ready to grill them.

7. Fire up a gas or charcoal grill to high heat. Place quail in a cast iron pan over direct heat, and cook for 3 minutes per side.

8. Move the pan to the coolest part of the grill and cook for another 10 minutes or until an instant-read thermometer inserted into the thigh registers 160 degrees. The meat will still look slightly pink.

Chef's Note: To cook the quail in the oven, preheat the oven to 475 degrees, and roast on each side for 8 minutes, or until an instant-read thermometer inserted into the thigh registers 160 degrees.

"Traditionally all you need for this dish is a can of jalapeños and a slab of bacon. Both items are built for the job and can go most anywhere without refrigeration. I usually break out this dish in October when fall is starting to take hold. It is a variation of an old hunter's classic done predominantly with dove. My variation of this dish is done with another small gamebird, quail. Small gamebirds benefit from a stuffing because of their size. A full serving of the stuffing helps to make more of a meal out of it." —CHEF BEN FORD

Bacon-Wrapped Maple Quail with Corn Succatash

CHEF DENNY CORRIVEAU | SERVES 6

12 quail breast halves

6 slices of applewood-smoked
   bacon, sliced into halves

2 ounces goat cheese

Wild Cheff Cinnamon Chile Blend

2 tablespoons pure maple syrup

½ teaspoon Wild Cheff
   Jalapeño Flakes

½ poblano pepper, seeded and
   veined, then thinly sliced

Corn Succotash (recipe following)

For the Corn Succotash

3 ears of sweet corn, sliced
   off the cob

1 small zucchini, cubed small

1 small red bell pepper, diced

1 poblano pepper, diced

2 tablespoons butter

1 tablespoon olive oil

½ tablespoon Wild Cheff Lemon
   Lover's Blend

1 teaspoon Wild Cheff Cajun
   Blend

1 teaspoon Wild Cheff Herb
   Lover's Blend

Sea salt, to taste

1. To prepare the succotash, heat a skillet over medium-high heat and add the olive oil and butter. Add veggies to the pan and begin to sauté. Season the veggies with the Wild Cheff spices and herbs and add sea salt to taste.

2. Stir veggies while cooking until they are al dente. You want them beyond the raw stage, but still slightly crisp. Put aside.

3. Place the breasts one at a time into a Ziploc bag. Using a meat mallet, gently tap the breasts to tenderize the meat and help it cook more evenly. Once they have been pounded into mini cutlets, place them into a medium-size mixing bowl. Pour Wild Cheff Blood Orange Olive Oil to coat the breasts, and season them with the Wild Cheff Cinnamon Chile Blend.

4. Place the goat cheese into a mixing bowl with the maple syrup and the Wild Cheff Jalapeño Flakes, and using a spatula, stir everything together until well blended.

5. Lay the bacon slices out on a cutting board. Place one seasoned quail breast on each half-slice of bacon. With a small spoon, place a dollop of the goat cheese mixture on the center of each breast, then place a poblano slice on top. Working one at a time, fold each breast over the cheese stuffing, then wrap with a piece of bacon, securing this with a toothpick.

6. In a preheated cast iron pan, add the bacon-wrapped breasts and cook, while turning, until the bacon is cooked and browned.

To Serve: Place the stuffed quail on a platter over the corn succotash.

Barbecue Bacon-Wrapped Quail

CHEF DEAN FEARING | SERVES 4

INGREDIENTS

4 quail, about 4 ounces each,
  semi-boneless
Salt and black pepper, to taste
8 strips jalapeño pepper, julienne
8 strips thin-sliced smoked bacon
1 cup warm barbecue sauce
  (use your favorite)
Jalapeño Ranch Dressing (recipe
  following)

For the Jalapeño Ranch Dressing

1 cup buttermilk
½ cup mayonnaise
⅓ cup jalapeño pepper,
  seeded and chopped
One 1-ounce package ranch
  dressing mix
Tabasco, to taste
Lime juice, to taste

1. Preheat oven to 375 degrees. On a clean cutting board, using a small chef knife, cut off the wing tips and legs from the quail. With the remaining boneless quail body, cut the back side of the quail (opposite of the breast meat) in the middle, lengthwise, to open up flat, skin side down. Repeat for each quail.

2. Season all sides of the quail with salt and pepper. Place two strips of jalapeño between the breasts. Starting on one side of the quail, roll into a tight cylinder. Repeat for each quail.

3. Lay two strips of bacon side by side. Place the quail at one end of the bacon. Roll into another tight cylinder with several rotations, making sure the bacon has completely covered the quail.

4. Place the quail 2 inches apart, seam side down, on a sheet pan. Put in the oven, and cook for 12 minutes, until the bacon has browned. Remove from the oven, and let rest for 5 minutes.

5. With a serrated knife, cut ½-inch rounds from the quail cylinder and place a skewer through the bacon. Dip the quail into the barbecue sauce to glaze.

6. For the Jalapeño Ranch Dressing, blend buttermilk, mayonnaise, jalapeño pepper, ranch dressing mix, Tabasco, and lime juice in a food processor or blender until mostly smooth.

To Serve: Serve warm with jalapeño ranch on the side for dipping.

Braised Duck with Turnips, Swiss Chard, and Dumplings

CHEF FRANK STITT | SERVES 4

INGREDIENTS

Four 8-ounce duck legs, wild or domestic, excess fat removed
Kosher salt and freshly ground black pepper
2 tablespoons canola oil
1 onion, finely chopped
1 carrot, peeled and finely chopped
2 celery stalks, finely chopped
1 cup red wine
2 cups chicken broth
3 thyme sprigs, 3 flat-leaf parsley sprigs, 2 bay leaves, and 1 leek top, tied together to make a bouquet garni
3–4 russet potatoes, cooked but still firm, skins removed
1 cup all-purpose flour
½ cup grated Parmesan cheese
4 egg yolks
Pinch of nutmeg
3 tablespoons unsalted butter
4 cipollini onions, peeled
4 baby turnips, quartered
¾ cup Swiss chard, trimmed, washed, and chopped

1. Preheat the oven to 300 degrees. In a large cast iron skillet, heat the canola oil. Season the duck legs with salt and pepper, and sear over medium-high heat, turning occasionally, until golden brown on all sides, about 15 minutes. Transfer to a rack set over a baking sheet to rest while preparing braise.

2. Add the onion, carrot, and celery to the skillet to cook, stirring occasionally, until well caramelized, about 15 minutes. Add the red wine, and simmer until the liquid has reduced by half. Add the chicken broth and garni, and bring to a boil. Place the duck legs in a casserole or baking dish and pour the braising liquid and vegetables over the legs. Place a piece of parchment paper directly on the duck and cover the casserole with the lid or aluminum foil. Place in the oven to cook at a gentle simmer for 45 to 75 minutes, or until tender: the meat should offer very little resistance when stuck with a fork.

3. Combine potatoes, ¾ cup flour, ¼ cup Parmesan, egg yolks, and nutmeg in a ricer or food mill. Using a spatula, fold remaining flour into the dough and stir until just sticky. Remove plastic wrap from dough, dust surface with a pinch of flour, and form a loaf, then set aside to rest, covered with plastic wrap, about 5 minutes. Dust surface with a pinch of flour and cut loaf into 1-by-1 inch pieces. Fold pieces over a gnocchi paddle or fork and drop into boiling salted water, cooking until dumplings float to the surface, about 1 to 1½ minutes. Set aside on an oiled pan to cool.

4. Remove duck legs from the oven and allow the legs to rest in the braising liquid for 10 to 15 minutes and remove to a rack. Pull the meat from the bone and set aside. Strain the broth into a small saucepan and bring to a simmer over medium heat, skimming frequently, until reduced by half. Set aside and keep warm.

5. In large cast iron skillet, heat 1 tablespoon butter, sear gnocchi until golden brown, and set aside. Add 1 tablespoon butter, cipollini onions, and baby turnips and sauté until golden brown, about 3 minutes. Add the duck meat, Swiss chard, and reserved braising liquid and heat about 1 minute. Add the dumplings and remaining tablespoon of butter and season with salt and pepper.

To Serve: Place in serving bowls and garnish with truffles and remaining ¼ cup Parmesan.

"I continue to love cooking and eating birds—quail, wild duck (especially teal) and hope to hunt and cook some woodcock. I've never cooked wild hare and would look forward to that. Visiting England and France during the winter, you see butcher shops filled with wild game and that is really exciting. One of my fondest restaurant memories is from the Connaught Hotel in London, and having a variety of wild game offered." —CHEF FRANK STITT

Gamebirds in Red Wine Gravy

CHEF CHARLIE PALMER | SERVES 4

Chef's Note: Braising or stewing birds such as partridge, wood pigeon, and even quail is a great way to get the meat tender and keep it moist. Test the thighs of the birds, and once that flesh is tender enough, the rest will be cooked.

INGREDIENTS

4 small gamebirds: partridge, pigeon, dove, or quail

8 ounces bacon, diced to ¼ inch

Kosher salt and freshly ground black pepper

12 spring onion bulbs

4 cups small whole button mushrooms (quartered, if large)

1 tablespoon all-purpose flour

2 cups red wine

Sprig of fresh or pinch of dried thyme

1. Using a pair of kitchen shears, cut the backbones from the birds and reserve for use in stock. Using a sturdy knife, split each breast in half from top to bottom, cutting through the breastplate. Pat the birds dry with paper towels.

2. In a Dutch oven over medium-high heat, cook the bacon until crisp, 5 to 7 minutes. Transfer the bacon to a small bowl or plate, leaving the fat in the pan. Season the birds with salt and pepper, and place in the pan with the hot bacon fat, skin side down (or meat side down, if the birds are skinless), and sear. Shake the pan gently to distribute the cooking fat evenly under the birds. Add a little more cooking fat as needed, if the bacon was especially lean. Cook the birds until the skin or meat is lightly browned, no more than 2 minutes. Flip and cook on the bone sides. Transfer the browned birds to a plate, and set them aside.

3. Add the spring onions and mushrooms to the pot, stirring as they cook and scraping the bottom of the pot to loosen any bits stuck to the bottom. (The mushrooms will help deglaze the browned bits from the pot with the moisture they give off during cooking.) Sear the vegetables until they are slightly golden and the onions are about halfway to being completely tender, about 5 minutes.

4. Sprinkle the flour over the vegetables in the pot, and stir to incorporate them, and then pour in the red wine, add the reserved bacon and thyme, and stir to combine. Simmer gently until slightly thickened, 7 to 10 minutes.

5. Nestle the birds into the thickening sauce in a single layer (skin or meat side up), and add any juices that remain on the plate. Baste the birds with the sauce, cover, and cook until they have reached the desired doneness—anywhere from 10 to 20 minutes. If the juices have not thickened enough once the meat is tender, remove the meat, reduce the liquid to a sauce consistency, and then return the meat to the sauce. Remove and discard the thyme sprig. Taste and adjust the seasoning, if necessary (the bacon should have added enough salt for the dish).

To Serve: Serve with plenty of crusty bread or simple mashed potatoes to soak up as much of the sauce as possible.

Buffalo Pheasant Wonton Cups

CHEF SEAN FINLEY | SERVES 4

"Game is an underused resource in our country that a lot of people aren't familiar with. I think people can look at and adapt the everyday recipes for things like chicken and beef and relate them back to the game they're shooting and they can come up with some pretty palatable recipes they can fix at home for their families. The big turnoff for most people is they don't know how to cook game, or that it dries out. People need to look at cooking methods like braising or roasting with a little bit of liquid. I try to work with everyone visiting the lodges to let them know how to prepare all the different dishes and make them taste great."

—CHEF SEAN FINLEY

INGREDIENTS

½ cup mayonnaise
2 cups of diced smoked pheasant
¼ cup fine diced poblano pepper
⅓ cup chopped green onion
½ cup finely diced celery
1 teaspoon ground mustard
1 teaspoon celery salt
1 teaspoon favorite hot sauce
    per wonton cup
12 wonton wrappers
Thin-sliced green, red, and yellow
    bell peppers
Sriracha hot chili sauce

1. Preheat your oven to 350 degrees. Spray one side of each wonton wrapper with vegetable oil spray.

2. Press the wonton wrappers, oil-coated side down, into miniature muffin cup forms. Bake the wrappers 8 to 11 minutes, until golden brown. Remove from the forms and let them cool.

3. In a medium bowl, combine mayo, smoked pheasant, diced poblano, green onion, celery, ground mustard, and celery salt. Mix thoroughly with a rubber spatula.

4. Place the pheasant mixture back into the refrigerator to let the flavors mix and cool for 1 to 2 hours.

To Serve: Spoon 1 teaspoon hot sauce into the bottom of each wonton cup. Spoon pheasant mixture into each wonton cup, filling them. Garnish with tricolored bell pepper slices and 1 drop of Sriracha hot chili sauce. Serve immediately.

Chef's Note: The salad can be made two or three days ahead of time and kept in an airtight container in the refrigerator.

Chef Finley's notes for preparing smoked pheasant:

Seasoning: Season the cavity of the bird with salt and pepper. Stuff the cavity of the bird with a bundle of thyme, rosemary, lemon peel, orange peel, sage, 2 bay leaves, and a quarter of peeled red onion. Also stuff in 2 to 3 whole garlic cloves.

Cooking: Place the pheasant in a smoker at 225 degrees for 4 to 6 hours, until internal temperature of the bird reaches 160 degrees. Use pecan or apple wood chips for best flavor.

Preserving: After the bird is smoked, keep it refrigerated until use. You can also wrap it tightly with plastic wrap or vacuum seal and freeze for up to 6 months. Thaw and debone for use.

Crisp Boneless Duck

CHEF TIM CREEHAN | SERVES 4

INGREDIENTS

Two 4- to 5-pound Long
    Island ducks
¼ cup soy sauce
1 cup Madeira wine
3 cups Duck Stock (recipe
    following)
Mashed Boniato (recipe following)
Sautéed Baby Green Beans (recipe
    following)
4 fresh rosemary sprigs
Granulated garlic, to taste
Salt, to taste
Black pepper, to taste

1. Preheat oven to 400 degrees.
Brush the ducks with the soy
sauce, and season generously
with garlic, salt, and pepper.

2. Place on a rack in a roasting
pan, and roast for 1½ hours or
until the skin is brown and the legs
move freely. Let stand until cool.

3. Split the ducks lengthwise, and
place skin side down on a work
surface. Remove the back, rib, and
breast bones. Cut the skin on the
wing and leg bones and carefully
pull the bones out from the side.

4. Increase oven temperature
to 500 degrees.

5. Place the ducks skin side up on
the rack in the roasting pan. Roast
for 15 minutes or until the skin is
crisp. Remove ducks from the pan,
reserving pan drippings.

6. Place the roasting pan over
high heat on the stove top; add
wine and duck stock. Cook until
reduced to desired consistency.

FOR THE DUCK STOCK

4 duck carcasses
1½ large yellow onions
1 celery rib
1½ large carrots
Leftover duck meat (optional)
1½ garlic bulbs
1 sprig fresh parsley
2 cups red wine
½ cup white wine
1 cup tomato paste
1 tablespoon black peppercorns
2 sprigs fresh thyme
2 bay leaves
2 tablespoons salt

1. Preheat oven to 450 degrees.
Place the bones on a baking sheet
and roast until brown on all sides.
Cut the onions, celery, and carrots
into large pieces. Combine the
chopped vegetables, bones, meat,
and remaining ingredients with
enough water to fill a 5-gallon
stockpot within 4 inches of the
top. Bring to a slow, rolling boil.

2. Cook 6 hours, skimming surface frequently. Remove from heat
and strain through a fine sieve or
chinois. Let stand to cool.

FOR THE MASHED BONIATO

2 pounds peeled boniato
    potatoes
1 gallon water
1 stick butter
1⅓ cups milk
⅓ cup sour cream
1 tablespoon salt
1 teaspoon white pepper

1. Cut the potatoes into small
pieces. Bring the water to a boil
in a large saucepan and add

potatoes. Cook 45 minutes or
until tender; drain completely.

2. Melt the butter with the milk in
a small saucepan. Combine with
the potatoes, sour cream, salt, and
pepper in a bowl. Mix with a firm
whisk until smooth.

FOR THE SAUTÉED BABY GREEN BEANS

1 quart water
Large bunch fresh french baby
    green beans
1 tablespoon butter
Chopped garlic, to taste
Salt, to taste
Black pepper, to taste

1. Bring the water to a boil in
a medium saucepan and add the
beans. Blanch just until tender-
crisp, and drain.

2. Melt the butter in a large sauté
pan; add the beans and garlic.
Sauté until just heated through.
Season with salt and pepper.

To Serve: Spoon the boniato onto
serving plates. Top with duck and
spoon reduced sauce over the top.
Garnish with baby green beans,
and a rosemary sprig.

Ragout of Quail with Summer Vegetables and Basil Pesto

CHEF GORDON HAMERSLEY | SERVES 2-4

INGREDIENTS

4 quail, dressed
3 tablespoons olive oil
1 tablespoon unsalted butter
8 pearl onions, skinned
3 cloves fresh garlic, skinned
   and chopped
1 red bell pepper, cored and diced
1 medium zucchini, diced
½ cup dry white wine
1 cup tomato juice
8 cherry tomatoes
1 small bunch green beans,
   stemmed and cut into
   2-inch pieces
1 small bunch snap peas
Basil Pesto (recipe following)

1. Preheat the oven to 350 degrees.

2. Wash the quail, and dry them well. Season with salt and black pepper.

3. In a heavy skillet, heat 3 tablespoons of olive oil and 1 tablespoon of unsalted butter. When the butter stops bubbling, add the quail, breast side down, and cook about 3 to 5 minutes, or until golden brown. Cook the other side until also golden brown. Remove the quail from the pan, and reserve.

4. Lower the heat to medium, and add the onions, garlic, pepper, and zucchini to the pan. Stir the vegetables, and cook for about 5 minutes. Add the white wine and tomato juice, and bring to a boil. Add the reserved quail back to the pan. Cover, and place into the oven. Cook for 25 minutes.

5. Add the cherry tomatoes, green beans, and snap peas to the pan and return this pan to the oven. Cook for an additional 10 minutes.

FOR THE BASIL PESTO

2 cups basil leaves, washed
   and dried
3 cloves garlic, skinned
¼ cup pine nuts, toasted
⅔ cup olive oil
½ teaspoon salt
½ cup grated Parmesan

1. To make the pesto, place the basil, garlic, and pine nuts into a food processor. Pulse until the basil begins to break down.

2. With the motor running, add the olive oil and salt. Place the basil mixture into a small bowl. Fold in the Parmesan cheese. Reserve.

To Serve: Divide the vegetables among four plates. Place the birds on top of the vegetables, and serve with pesto on the side.

"I will never forget the first time when hunting quail, and 15 or so blasted out in front of me. I'm getting better at focusing on one bird when that happens now, and I hopefully bring one down... But the panic never really leaves me."

—CHEF GORDON HAMERSLEY

Pheasant Applejack

CHEF DENNY CORRIVEAU | SERVES 4-6

INGREDIENTS

6 boneless pheasant breast halves

Wild Cheff Lemon Olive Oil

Wild Cheff Tuscan Blend

Organic all-purpose flour, for
dredging

2 to 3 tablespoons of butter

1 apple, peeled, cored, and
diced small

½ tablespoon Wild Cheff
Air-Dried Shallots

½ teaspoon of Wild Cheff Pie
Spice Blend

¾ cup of apple brandy (not
schnapps)

½ cup of apple cider

1. Place the pheasant breast halves, one at a time, into a 1-quart Ziploc bag. Very gently pound the breasts with a meat mallet so they are thin, like a cutlet. As you finish each, remove from bag, and place on a large plate. When all the breasts are finished and prepared, drizzle Wild Cheff Lemon Olive Oil over them so they are fully coated. Season them with desired amount of Wild Cheff Tuscan Blend.

2. Dredge the breasts in the flour, and shake off the excess. Place them onto a new, clean plate to prep them for cooking. Preheat a large cast iron or stainless sauté pan with olive oil and 1 tablespoon butter over the stovetop on medium heat. Sauté the pheasant breasts in the oil on each side until almost fully cooked. Transfer the cooked pheasant to a plate, and loosely cover with aluminum foil.

3. Add a tablespoon of butter to the pan. Once it melts, add the diced apples and Wild Cheff Air-Dried Shallots, followed by the Wild Cheff Pie Spice Blend. Stir to incorporate the flavors.

4. When the apples appear to have softened, add the apple brandy to the pan. Be careful not to expose the brandy to open flame, as it will ignite the brandy and flame up.

5. Cook for 1 to 2 minutes and then add the apple cider to the pan. Continue to sauté, and add another tablespoon of butter to the pan if needed, and you will see the sauce start to thicken up.

6. Add the pheasant cutlets back to the pan and coat them in the sauce, then serve.

Chef's Note: Suggested side dishes include a fall squash and wild rice or your favorite potatoes.

Fried Chicken Livers

CHEF FRANK STITT | SERVES 4

INGREDIENTS

12 fresh chicken livers (or rabbit), trimmed, cleaned, and cut in half
½ cup buttermilk
⅓ cup peanut oil
1 small shallot, finely minced
1 tablespoon Dijon mustard
2 tablespoons Noble bourbon sherry vinegar (or 2 tablespoons sherry vinegar with 1 tablespoon Maker's Mark)
⅓ cup extra-virgin olive oil
1 cup cornmeal
1 cup flour
1 cup cooked grits, cooked with water, butter, and Parmesan cheese
2 cups frisée lettuce or a mixture of soft and bitter lettuces
¼ pound slab bacon, cut into thick lardoons, cooked until just crisp, fat reserved
Salt, freshly ground black pepper, and cayenne pepper, to taste

1. Soak the livers in a bowl with buttermilk for 30 minutes. In a cast iron skillet, heat peanut oil to 360 degrees; you want the peanut oil to be 2 inches deep.

2. Make a vinaigrette by combining the shallots, salt, black pepper, Dijon mustard, and vinegar, and whisk in the olive oil and remaining bacon fat; adjust seasonings.

3. Combine the cornmeal, flour, salt, pepper, and cayenne in a mixing bowl. Remove the livers from the buttermilk and coat with the cornmeal mixture. Carefully place into the hot oil and fry until crisp and rosy colored inside—about 4 minutes. Do not over- or under-cook. Drain on paper towels.

To Serve: Toss the frisée with the vinaigrette, and place around the warm, soft grits. Top with chicken livers and bacon, and serve with a little more of the vinaigrette.

Duck Stir Fry

CHEF SCOTT LEYSATH | SERVES 4

INGREDIENTS

2 cups skinless duck breast filets, thinly sliced across the grain

½ gallon water

½ cup Kosher salt

½ cup brown sugar

1 tablespoon cornstarch

¼ cup ponzu soy sauce (a low-sodium, citrus-infused soy sauce)

½ teaspoon sesame oil

3 tablespoons vegetable or peanut oil

4 green onions, roughly chopped

1 cup celery, thinly sliced

1 cup carrots, thinly sliced

2 cups baby bok choy, halved or shredded cabbage

2 tablespoons pickled ginger, minced

¼ cup unagi sauce (available in Japanese markets, many grocery stores, or through online suppliers)

1 teaspoon Sriracha, or other hot sauce

1. First, brine the duck by combining ½ gallon water with ½ cup Kosher salt or any coarse salt, and brown sugar. Heat a cup or two of water and salt in a saucepan until the salt is dissolved. Cool, and add to remaining water. Place ducks or duck parts in the brine for 6 to 12 hours. Rinse, pat dry, and proceed with your favorite recipe. As with any stir-fry, it's essential that all ingredients are prepped and ready for fast cooking. Do not overcook your duck.

2. In a bowl, combine sliced duck breast with cornstarch, ponzu, and sesame oil and toss to coat evenly. Smooth out any lumps.

3. Heat the oil in a medium-hot skillet or wok. Add the marinated duck breast and quickly stir-fry for 1 minute. Add remaining ingredients and stir-fry for 2 to 3 minutes more.

To Serve: Serve over warm, cooked rice or noodles.

"Wild-game home cooks routinely go to extraordinary lengths to mask the taste of wild game. They've been told that no game shall be prepared without a lengthy soak in some concoction aimed at driving out the evil gamey spirits. After someone recites a recipe, they often end with, 'It's so good, it doesn't even taste like duck,' which to me is not a victory. I can't say that I blame them. There's a good chance that they were raised on overcooked wild meats that tasted muttony, livery, and gamey. If my duck tasted like liver, I'd try to cover it up too! Waterfowl benefits from a good soak in a simple saltwater brine." —**CHEF SCOTT LEYSATH**

Marinated Spatchcocked Quail

CHEF CHARLIE PALMER | SERVES 4

INGREDIENTS

8 quail, 4 to 6 ounces each
2 shallots, finely chopped
4 garlic cloves, minced
2 teaspoons dried oregano,
   crushed
¼ cup fresh lemon juice
2 teaspoons Kosher salt
½ cup olive oil
Pinch of cayenne pepper
Freshly ground black pepper
Kosher salt, to taste
Lemon wedges, for garnish
White Bean Ragout (recipe
   following)

1. Using a pair of heavy kitchen or poultry shears, snip the wing tips from the quail and cut out the backbone from each bird. Open and press down on each bird so the skin side rests flat.

2. In a small nonreactive bowl, mix together all of the ingredients for the marinade. Spoon a quarter of the marinade into the bottom of a shallow nonreactive container that is large enough to hold all of the flattened birds in a single layer. Place the quail in the container, skin side up.

3. Pour the rest of the marinade over the birds, pressing them down with your fingertips to make sure all the surfaces are covered with the marinade. Cover with plastic wrap, and refrigerate the quail for at least 4 hours, preferably overnight.

4. Remove the quail from the marinade, and grill over medium-high heat for 2 to 3 minutes per side. Let rest for 5 minutes, then sprinkle with salt.

FOR THE WHITE BEAN RAGOUT

4 ounces slab pancetta, diced
1 pound white beans, picked over,
   rinsed, and soaked overnight in
   plenty of fresh water
4 cups chicken stock or water
2 garlic cloves, smashed
Pinch of crushed red chili flakes
Pinch of dried thyme
2 bay leaves
1 medium onion, cut into large dice
1 cup carrot, cut into large dice
1 cup coarsely chopped celery
1½ teaspoons Kosher salt
Freshly ground black pepper

1. Heat a 4-quart Dutch oven over medium heat. Add the pancetta and cook, stirring, until it is golden brown and crisp, and the fat is released; this will take about 5 minutes.

2. Drain the soaked beans and discard the soaking liquid; rinse the beans, and add them to the Dutch oven along with the chicken stock or water, garlic, chili flakes, thyme, and bay leaves. Bring to a simmer, lower the heat, and cover. Simmer until the beans are three-quarters of the way done, about 30 minutes.

3. Stir the onion, carrot, celery, salt, and pepper into the beans and continue to cook, uncovered, until all of the ingredients, including the beans, are tender, another 20 minutes or so. Remove and discard the bay leaves.

To Serve: Plate the Spatchcocked quail with the White Bean Ragout, and serve quail with lemon wedges.

"The term 'spatchcock' refers to the method of removing the backbone of quail (or other poultry) with poultry shears, then breaking the breastbone and flattening the bird with the palm of your hand."

—CHEF CHARLIE PALMER

Pheasant Burger

CHEF SEAN FINLEY | SERVES 4

INGREDIENTS

2 pounds ground pheasant meat
4 cloves minced fresh garlic
¼ cup finely diced roasted
   poblano chili
¼ cup minced red onion
1 teaspoon crushed red
   pepper flakes
2 tablespoons yellow
   curry powder
1 teaspoon Kosher salt
1 teaspoon table ground
   black pepper
¾ cup honey
Wasabi Mayo (recipe following)
Hand-cut Fries (recipe following)

1. Combine all ingredients except mayo and fries to create the pheasant burger mix.

2. Make pheasant mix into individual balls, about 5 ounces each. Place onto a hot flat griddle, smash out with a metal spatula to form a uniform patty and fry until the patty is lightly browned. Then flip and fry the second side of the patty to a light golden brown.

3. Remove the patties to a baking pan lined with parchment paper pre-seasoned with olive oil, salt, and pepper. Evenly distribute the patties on the pan and add a thin layer of chicken stock to the pan (which helps to braise the patties in the roasting process and keeps them moist). Roast at 400 degrees for 8 to 10 minutes until the patties are cooked through, with an internal temperature of 160 degrees or greater.

Chef's note: To save time, the burger mix can be prepared the night before, allowing the mixture to set up overnight in a cold refrigerator.

FOR THE WASABI MAYO

1 teaspoon prepared wasabi paste
1 cup mayonnaise

Combine the wasabi paste and mayonnaise together in a small mixing bowl. If the dressing is too spicy for your liking, cut back on the amount of wasabi paste.

FOR THE HAND-CUT FRIES

4 Idaho russet potatoes
Peanut oil, for frying

1. Cut the fries ahead of time into ¼-inch strips and wash them in cold water until the water runs clear, to remove all the starch from the potato. Dry them thoroughly in a towel before frying them in the hot oil, at 350 degrees.

2. After the initial frying of 4 to 7 minutes, allow the fries to rest and then re-fry them for 2 to 3 minutes before service. This will put a nice crisp on the outside and keep the inside soft.

To Serve: Serve on a toasted Hawaiian bun built from the bottom up with wasabi mayo, romaine lettuce, sliced tomato, sliced red onion, and a big handful of hand-cut fries on the side.

Pheasant Leg Stew

CHEF SCOTT LEYSATH | SERVES 8-10

Chef's Note: Any recipe for a stew should be used as an outline, a starting point from which you simmer a palatable blend of protein, vegetables, and stock. Adding a starchy component like potatoes or rice will add body to an otherwise brothy pot of stew.

INGREDIENTS

2 cups braised pheasant, shredded (recipe following)
5 cups pheasant or chicken stock (recipe following)
½ cup butter
1 cup carrot, peeled and diced
1 cup celery, diced
1 cup yellow onion, diced
3 garlic cloves, minced
½ cup flour
2 cups mushrooms, thinly sliced
2 cups whole milk (or substitute an additional 2 cups stock)
1 cup cooked wild rice
Salt and pepper

1. Melt half the butter in a large stockpot over medium heat. Add carrots, celery, yellow onion, and garlic cloves, and cook until onions are translucent.

2. Add the rest of the butter. When melted, sprinkle flour over the vegetables, and stir often, cooking for 3 minutes. Stir in ½ cup stock and continue stirring until smooth. Add remaining stock, a little at a time, while stirring.

3. Add mushrooms and milk (if you want it a little creamy), bring to a boil, and simmer for 10 minutes. Stir in rice and shredded pheasant. Season to taste with salt and pepper.

FOR THE BRAISE

10 to 12 pheasant legs
1 large onion, diced
4 celery stalks, diced
4 carrots, diced

1. Brown the pheasant legs in a large lightly-oiled, heavy-duty, oven-safe stock pot. Add diced onion, celery, and carrot. Continue the browning process until the onions are translucent.

2. Remove the pheasant legs, and add about 1 inch of liquid—wine, broth, water, or a combination—and stir to deglaze bits stuck to the pot.

3. Return browned pheasant legs to the pot, cover, and place in a 325-degree oven, making sure that there is always at least ¾- to 1-inch of liquid in the pot.

4. After 3 hours, test for doneness. Meat will fall off the bones when done. Cool, and remove the meat.

Chef's Note: Braising is much the same process that most people use with their slow-cookers. Tough cuts of meat are first browned before slow simmering them in a shallow pool of flavorful liquid in a covered container. This is a great way to turn pheasant legs and thighs into tender vittles. After several hours in a low-temperature oven, otherwise tough muscles can be easily pulled away from the bones. Best of all, braising can be done well in advance and in mass quantities. Save the legs and carcasses in the freezer until ready to use and braise them all at once.

FOR THE STOCK

1. Return picked leg and thigh bones to the braising pot. Add additional celery, carrots, onions, along with a few garlic cloves, a bay leaf or two, and, if available, a few sprigs of fresh herbs.

2. Cover the contents of the pot with cold water. Bring to a low boil, then reduce the heat to low and simmer, uncovered, for several hours.

3. Pour contents of the pot through a colander to remove large pieces. Discard contents of colander, line the colander with cheesecloth or paper towels, and pour liquid through the colander to clarify the stock.

Pheasant on Red Cabbage and Cranberries with Roasted Vegetables and Wilted Spinach

CHEF TIM CREEHAN | SERVES 4

INGREDIENTS

2 pheasants, dressed
2 pounds red cabbage, rinsed and finely shredded
2 medium onions, peeled and thinly sliced
1 tablespoon brown sugar
1 tablespoon black currant jelly
1 teaspoon ground cinnamon
⅓ cup fresh cranberries
2 apples, cored and chopped (but not peeled)
1 pinch dry mustard
¾ cup red wine vinegar
2 cups water
Salt, to taste
Freshly ground black pepper, to taste
¼ cup melted butter
2 cloves garlic, pressed
6 slices bacon

For the Roasted Vegetables

½ small butternut squash, peeled and cut into strips
1 sweet potato, peeled and cut into strips
1 Yukon Gold potato, washed and sliced ½-inch thick
½ tablespoon chopped fresh thyme
½ tablespoon chopped fresh rosemary
2 tablespoons olive oil
1 tablespoon balsamic vinegar
Salt, to taste
Freshly ground black pepper, to taste

For the Wilted Spinach

1 tablespoon extra-virgin olive oil
1 pound fresh spinach, stemmed and rinsed
Salt, to taste
Ground black pepper, to taste

1. In a heavy-bottomed saucepan over medium-low heat, combine cabbage, onions, sugar, jelly, cinnamon, cranberries, apples, mustard, vinegar, and water. Season to taste with salt and pepper.

2. Cover and cook 2 to 3 hours or until mixture is thickened, stirring occasionally. If too much liquid remains, uncover and boil rapidly, stirring occasionally, until the liquid is reduced.

3. Preheat oven to 450 degrees.

4. While cabbage is cooking, brush pheasant with melted butter, and season with salt, pepper, and garlic. Place birds, breast side up, in a roasting pan.

5. Lay bacon slices over the top, and bake 20 minutes, basting frequently with melted butter. Reduce temperature to 350 degrees. Cover, and cook 50 minutes.

6. Remove cover, and roast bird for an additional 45 minutes or until golden brown and moist, basting frequently with pan juices. Remove pheasant from oven, and cut into serving pieces.

7. Meanwhile, in a large bowl, combine the squash, sweet potato, and Yukon Gold potato. In a small bowl, stir together thyme, rosemary, olive oil, vinegar, salt, and pepper. Toss with vegetables until they are coated. Spread evenly on a large roasting pan.

8. Roast for 45 to 55 minutes in the preheated oven, stirring every 10 minutes, or until vegetables are cooked through and browned.

9. Heat oil in a large skillet over medium-high heat. Add spinach, and toss until just wilted, about 2 minutes. Season with salt and pepper to taste.

To Serve: Divide red cabbage and cranberries among plates. Layer roasted vegetables, wilted spinach, sliced pheasant, and bacon.

Quail and Waffles

CHEF SCOTT OSTRANDER | SERVES 8

INGREDIENTS

8 quail, dressed
½ cup pickle brine
½ cup Louisiana Hot Sauce
Seasoned flour, for frying
2 cups Cornbread Waffle Batter
   (recipe following)
1 cup Southern Pepper Jelly
   (recipe following)

1. If the quail are whole, prepare them by splitting in half and removing the backbone (and breastbone if a boneless breast is desired—otherwise leave intact).

2. Marinate the quail with the pickle brine and hot sauce, and allow to sit for at least 4 hours. Heat a waffle iron or electric waffle machine, and add the cornbread batter according to the manufacturer's instructions. You should have one small waffle per person (or a quarter of a Belgian waffle).

3. Remove the quail from the brine and dredge in seasoned flour. Using a heavy sauté pan with ½ inch of cooking oil, pan fry the quail until done.

FOR THE CORNBREAD WAFFLE BATTER

½ cup cornmeal
1 cup all-purpose flour
2 teaspoons baking powder
½ teaspoon salt
6 tablespoons sugar
5 tablespoons melted butter
1 tablespoon vegetable oil
2 eggs
4 ounces milk

In a large bowl, whip the eggs until fluffy. Add the milk, whisk to combine, and then incorporate the dry ingredients. Add the butter and oil, and whisk until just mixed.

FOR THE SOUTHERN PEPPER JELLY

1 red bell pepper, minced
4 jalapeño peppers, seeded and minced
1 teaspoon ground paprika
¼ teaspoon ground cayenne
½ teaspoon crushed red pepper
½ cup white vinegar
2½ cups white sugar
1½ teaspoons apple pectin powder

Combine all ingredients in a saucepan over medium heat and bring just to a boil. Whisk to dissolve sugar, transfer to a one-quart container, and allow to cool.

To Serve: Serve the quail over the waffles, and drizzle with the Southern Pepper Jelly.

"I marinate the quail in a brine of pickle juice and hot sauce, which adds tenderness. Diners come here looking for something a little different. A lot of them, especially the men, order our game dishes, which go well with the hunting lodge theme and mountain setting."

—CHEF SCOTT OSTRANDER

Pheasant Street Taco

CHEF SCOTT LEYSATH | YIELDS 12 SMALL TACOS

INGREDIENTS

1⅓ cups shredded braised pheasant leg and thigh meat (recipe on page 148)

¼ teaspoon Kosher salt

¼ teaspoon ground coriander

Pinch ground cumin

Pinch cayenne pepper

¼ cup fresh cilantro leaves, chopped

2 tablespoons olive oil

⅓ cup sour cream

2 tablespoons lime juice

Pinch sugar

24 small corn tortillas, quickly browned in a hot skillet

¼ cup Cotija cheese (or any other cheese you prefer)

⅔ cup pico de gallo (or a favorite salsa)

2 cups shredded lettuce

2 radishes, julienned

1. In a bowl, combine the braised pheasant with salt, coriander, cumin, pepper, and cilantro leaves, and mix well. Heat oil in a large skillet over medium heat, add the pheasant mixture and cook, stirring often, until hot.

2. Whisk together sour cream, lime juice, and sugar.

To Serve: Arrange warm corn tortillas, two stacked per serving, on a work surface. Top each with pheasant mixture, pico de gallo, shredded lettuce, cheese, and radishes. Drizzle the sour cream mixture over each.

Chef's Note: Here we have yet another example of how smaller is sometimes better. Street tacos were so-named by Americans after they were discovered being served by street vendors across Mexico. Smallish corn tortillas are doubled to keep the filling from falling onto the street while being eaten standing up. It's street food, and it's delicious. This version is a tad more Americanized than your basic street food, and what you put in your street taco is obviously a matter of personal choice. If pulled leg and thigh pheasant meat is not available, cooked and shredded breast filets will do the trick.

Quail Egg Pizza

CHEF GIANNI GALLUCCI | YIELDS ONE 12-INCH PIZZA

INGREDIENTS

8.8 ounces Neapolitan pizza dough
  (recipe following)
3 ounces San Marzano
  tomato purée
3 ounces cooked quail, shredded
5 basil leaves
4 ounces fresh mozzarella, cubed
3 ounces pancetta or bacon
4 quail eggs
Grated Pecorino Romano
Freshly ground black pepper,
  to taste
Candied cherries
1 ounce extra-virgin olive oil

1. Stretch out dough ball to the desired size (roughly 12 inches, preferably as round as possible). With a spoon, spread the tomato purée. Add shredded quail, basil, fresh mozzarella, and pancetta.

2. Crack the quail eggs, and distribute them evenly over the pizza, keeping the yolks intact. Sprinkle fresh Pecorino and black pepper over the entire pizza. Add the candied cherries, and place in oven.

3. Bake at 475 degrees until cheese has melted. Remove from oven, and drizzle with extra-virgin olive oil and serve. (For wood-burning ovens, cook at 800 degrees for about 90 seconds and remove.)

FOR THE NEAPOLITAN PIZZA DOUGH

(yields 12, 250-gram [8.8-ounce]
  dough balls)
1 kilogram (2.2 pounds) water,
  chilled
50 grams (1.76 ounces) sea salt
1.65 kilograms (3.64 pounds)
  Caputo 00 flour
1 gram (0.035 ounces) fresh yeast

1. Place salt in bowl, and pour 60 percent of water in bowl, stirring to dissolve the salt. Slowly mix in half the flour.

2. In a separate bowl, mix yeast with remaining water. Pour this into flour mixture, then mix in remaining flour to form a dough. Let rest for one hour, covered, then form into separate balls.

3. Store covered dough at room temperature. It will be ready to use in 18 hours.

Chef's Note: This dough recipe is very precise and requires a kitchen scale.

"It was something as simple as a pizza which could make us forget about the bad times in life and just focus on friendships. People in Italy eat pizza almost more for a social reason than actually being hungry. In America they say, 'Hey, let's get a coffee and catch up,' but in Naples they say, 'Hey, let's grab a pizza and talk.'"

—CHEF GIANNI GALLUCCI

Roasted Quail with Peas, Morels, and Parmesan Risotto

CHEF GORDON HAMERSLEY | SERVES 2-4

INGREDIENTS

4 quail, dressed
Kosher salt, to taste
Freshly ground black pepper,
   to taste
4 sprigs tarragon
2 tablespoons butter
1 tablespoon canola oil
4–6 cups chicken or vegetable
   stock
1 cup dry white wine
1 small white onion, finely chopped
2 cloves garlic, minced
8–10 fresh morels, or dried morels
   soaked in warm water
   and drained
1 cup Arborio rice
2 cups fresh or frozen peas
3 scallions, white parts and 2
   inches of green tops, thinly
   sliced
1 teaspoon lemon zest
½ cup grated Parmesan cheese

1. Preheat oven to 350 degrees. Rinse the quail, and dry thoroughly. Sprinkle with salt and black pepper and stuff the cavity of each with a sprig of tarragon.

2. Heat the butter and canola oil in a heavy-bottomed sauté pan until the butter stops bubbling. Add the quail, breast side down, and cook until golden brown. Turn and cook on the other side until also golden brown.

3. Place the pan in the oven, and cook for an additional 8 to 10 minutes, or until the quail is just cooked through. Remove the quail from the pan, and place on an oven-proof platter. Keep warm while making the risotto, for which you will use the sauté pan.

4. Heat the stock and white wine in a small saucepan until it boils. Turn off the heat.

5. Add the onion, garlic, and morels to the sauté pan in which the quail were cooked. Cook over medium heat for 3 minutes. Add the rice, and stir to coat with the vegetables.

6. Add 1 cup of warm broth to the pan and stir gently until most of the liquid is absorbed. Add another cup of warm broth and continue to stir until absorbed. Continue cooking the rice in this way until about 3 to 4 cups of stock have been used. Season the rice with salt, to taste.

7. Add the peas and scallions and 1 cup of broth to the pan. Stir until the broth has been absorbed. Test the rice. If it is still quite hard, add more broth until the rice is just barely tender. Add ¼ cup of Parmesan cheese and stir to combine. Add the lemon zest, and stir to combine.

To Serve: Divide the rice among warm pasta bowls. Place a quail on top of the rice, and sprinkle with the remaining cheese.

Roasted Quail with Pheasant Sausage Stuffing

CHEF SCOTT LEYSATH | SERVES 4

"I grew up in Virginia when standard quail-hunting protocol was searching for promising hedgerows and brier patches. We'd find the landowners and assure them that all gates would be closed, no livestock would be liberated, and, if needed, we would help with any heavy lifting or grunt work as repayment. We didn't have dogs, just a good sense of where bobwhites like to hang out, and we could always find enough rocks to scare them out of a brush pile or berry thicket. I've since never been without at least two setters, either English or Gordon." —CHEF SCOTT LEYSATH

INGREDIENTS

8 quail, whole
1½ cups pheasant breast, cooked and minced
⅓ cup smoky bacon, cooked and minced
¼ cup red onion, minced
2 garlic cloves, minced
1 medium jalapeño pepper, seeded and minced
¼ teaspoon Kosher salt
Pinch freshly ground black pepper
¼ teaspoon dried oregano leaves
1 large egg
Kosher salt and pepper, to taste
8 lemon slices

1. Preheat oven to 350 degrees. Season the quail liberally with salt and pepper. In a bowl, combine the rest of the ingredients (except for the lemon slices), and mix well to form a stuffing. Divide the stuffing in half, and then halve again, and then one more time, making eight equal portions. Roll each into a ball, and place one inside each quail for roasting.

2. Place stuffed quail, breast side up, on a lightly greased baking sheet and place a lemon slice over each. Roast in the preheated oven for 12 to 15 minutes, or until golden brown.

Chef's Note: This is a great way to stretch a few upland birds into dinner and makes good use of an older and "toothier" rooster for the stuffing. If you are adept at boning out a quail while keeping the body intact, it will allow for additional stuffing.

Vermont Pheasant with Sundried Bing Cherry and Applejack Brandy Sauce

CHEF DOUG MACK | SERVES 2

INGREDIENTS

1 pheasant, plucked, cleaned, legs and breasts removed
1 cup white wine
½ cup oil
1 teaspoon tarragon
1 teaspoon chopped garlic
1 teaspoon chopped parsley
White wine (additional for roasting)
Sundried Bing Cherry and Applejack Brandy Sauce (recipe following)

1. For the marinade, combine the wine, ½ cup oil, tarragon, garlic, and parsley in a large bowl. Marinate the pheasant breasts and legs for 1 hour before cooking, keeping them refrigerated.

2. Preheat the oven to 350 degrees. Roast the marinated breasts and legs in a little wine for about 15 minutes. Remove the breasts; roast the legs for another 15 minutes. Keep all the pheasant warm while making the brandy sauce.

3. In a pan, sauté the breasts, only, in a little oil, heating the oil until hot before adding the breasts; this helps keep them from sticking to the bottom of the pan. Cook the breasts 3 minutes per side.

FOR THE SUNDRIED BING CHERRY AND APPLEJACK BRANDY SAUCE

½ cup sundried cherries (soaked for 4 hours in warm water) or fresh cherries
1 cup mushrooms
1 ounce oil or butter
½ cup applejack brandy
1 teaspoon flour
1½ cups chicken stock
1 tablespoon chopped parsley

1. Sauté the cherries and mushrooms in oil. When the mushrooms are soft, add the brandy.

2. Simmer for 1 minute, then add the flour, and simmer for another 2 minutes. Add the stock and parsley, and simmer for 15 minutes longer.

To Serve: Slice the breasts into thin strips cut on the bias, place in a small pool of prepared sauce, and fan out. Prior to serving, reheat the legs in the oven for 10 minutes. Serve the legs alongside the sliced breasts.

Ginger Citrus Baked Woodcock

CHEF DENNY CORRIVEAU | SERVES 2

INGREDIENTS

4 woodcock, dressed
Wild Cheff Blood Orange
    Olive Oil
Wild Cheff Lemon Pepper Spice
    Blend, to taste
4 tablespoons of butter
2 teaspoons of Wild Cheff Ginger
    Citrus Spice Blend
½ cup of orange juice
¼ cup of water
½ cup of Beaujolais wine
1 teaspoon of orange zest
1 cup of seedless red grapes

1. Preheat oven to 350 degrees. Coat birds with Wild Cheff Blood Orange Olive Oil and then add desired amount of Wild Cheff Lemon Pepper Spice Blend to inside and outside of birds. Place them into a baking dish that has been lightly coated with olive oil.

2. In a saucepan, heat butter, Wild Cheff Ginger Citrus Spice Blend, orange juice, water, wine, orange zest, and grapes, until sauce thickens.

3. Pour sauce over the birds and cook for 45 to 50 minutes, basting with sauce every 10 minutes.

To Serve: Serve with wild rice, studded with dried fruit and seasonal veggies.

‹ Blackberry-Balsamic Glazed Quail

CHEF ANGELIA HIGHSMITH | SERVES 9

INGREDIENTS

18 quail, dressed
1 quart Fire & Flavor Espresso &
    Chili Brine
Blackberry-Balsamic Glaze (recipe
    following)

For the Blackberry-Balsamic Glaze

½ cup balsamic vinegar
½ cup red wine
¼ cup tamari sauce
¼ cup blackberry jelly
2 tablespoons Dijon mustard
1 tablespoon minced garlic

1. Soak quail in brine for 30 minutes.

2. To prepare the glaze, place all ingredients in a large non-aluminum pan and bring to a boil. Cook until volume is reduced by three-quarters. Cool to thicken.

3. Cook quail on grill to desired temperature at 165 degrees.

4. Just before quail is done, brush the glaze on liberally and let the heat set the glaze, being very careful not to burn it.

To Serve: Garnish with fresh blackberries, and serve.

"One should never assume that any wild game has had the ideal diet and conditions. When in doubt, use hunter's insurance: a brine. Brines force moisture and flavor into the meat. Whether you prepare it yourself or use one of Gina Knox's Fire & Flavor brines, they always make your game taste great!" —CHEF ANGELIA HIGHSMITH

Roasted Quail with Prosciutto, Red Onions, and Burnt Peaches

CHEF GORDON HAMERSLEY | SERVES 2-4

4 quail, dressed

1 red onion, cut in quarters

1 ripe peach, pit removed, cut
   in quarters

2 tablespoons canola oil

Salt and freshly ground black
   pepper, to taste

4 slices of prosciutto, thinly sliced

4 tablespoons aged sherry vinegar

½ cup chicken stock

3 tablespoons honey

2 tablespoons unsalted butter

Watercress or greens, for serving

1. Preheat the oven to 350 degrees.

2. Heat the canola oil in a roasting pan large enough to hold all the ingredients in a single layer. (If one pan is not large enough, use two—one for the peaches and onions, one for the quail.) Remove the pan from the heat and carefully place the red onions and the peach halves, cut side down, into the pan.

3. Wrap the prosciutto around the quail. Season with salt and pepper and place the birds into the roasting pan alongside the peaches and red onion.

4. Place the roasting pan in the oven for about 15 minutes, or until the quail are cooked through.

5. Remove the quail, peaches, and onions from the pan and arrange on a large platter. The onions should be tender and golden brown and the peaches should be dark brown. If necessary, cook them both cut side down on the stovetop until well colored. Decorate with the watercress or greens. Reserve.

6. Add the sherry vinegar, chicken stock, and honey to the pan, and bring to a boil on top of the stove. Season with salt to taste. Whisk in the butter, and pour over and around the quail.

Sautéed Quail

CHEF STEVEN SATTERFIELD | SERVES 4

INGREDIENTS

8 Manchester Farms semi-boneless quail
2 tablespoons olive oil
2 tablespoons butter
Kosher salt and milled black pepper
Acorn Squash Purée (recipe following)
Sautéed Kale and Apple (recipe following)

1. Rinse the quail and pat dry, tucking wings behind the breast. Heat a large sauté pan over high heat and add olive oil.

2. Season quail on both sides liberally with Kosher salt and black pepper and then place gently into the hot pan, breast side down.

3. Cook on high heat until the skin is golden brown, and then turn over and add butter to the pan. Allow butter to brown while the quail is cooking on the other side 1 or 2 more minutes.

4. Pull from heat and allow quail to rest.

FOR THE ACORN SQUASH PURÉE

1 acorn squash, halved and seeded
1 tablespoon apple cider vinegar
4 tablespoons butter
1 teaspoon sea salt
3 or 4 cloves of roasted garlic
½ to ¾ cup water or chicken stock

1. Roast squash at 350 degrees for 30 to 40 minutes, until tender. Allow to cool slightly and then remove the skin.

2. Place squash in a blender or food processor with remaining ingredients and blend until smooth, adding the water or stock a little at a time until it reaches the desired consistency. Taste, and season as needed.

Chef's Note: To roast garlic, wrap a garlic bulb in foil and cook at 300 degrees for 45 minutes or until tender.

FOR THE SAUTÉED KALE AND APPLE

2 tablespoons olive oil
1 tablespoon butter
2 bunches of kale, washed and stemmed
1 teaspoon garlic, chopped
1 teaspoon shallot, minced
1 tart apple, quartered, seeds removed, and thinly sliced
Salt and pepper, to taste

1. In a large sauté pan over medium heat, add butter and olive oil, shallots, and garlic. When they begin to sizzle, add the washed kale and season lightly. You may need to add a splash of water or chicken stock to keep the greens moist as they cook.

2. As the greens wilt, keep them turning in the pan. When the greens are tender, toss in raw apple to combine.

To Serve: For each serving, spoon ¼ cup of warm squash purée onto each plate and add greens and apple, and top with sautéed quail. Top with toasted pumpkin seeds, if desired.

Buttermilk Biscuits with Goose Breakfast Sausage

CHEF DAVID GUAS | SERVES 8-10

INGREDIENTS

2 cups all-purpose flour, chilled (preferably White Lily), plus more as needed

2 tablespoons baking powder

¾ teaspoons Kosher salt

½ cup unsalted butter, cold and cut into ½-inch pieces

2 tablespoons unsalted butter, melted

¾ cup buttermilk, plus more for brushing

Goose Breakfast Sausage (recipe following)

1. Position a rack in the center of the oven, and heat the oven to 375 degrees. Line a cookie sheet with parchment paper.

2. Chill a food processor blade and bowl, as well as a large mixing bowl. In the chilled food processor, pulse the flour, baking powder, and salt until combined. Add the cold butter, and process with ten 1-second pulses; the butter should be the size of small peas.

3. Transfer the mixture to the chilled mixing bowl. Add the buttermilk, moving your hand, with fingers apart, in circles to incorporate it into the dry ingredients. The dough is mixed when it just barely comes together.

4. Transfer the dough to a lightly floured work surface. Pat and roll it into a ½ inch-thick square. Using a floured 2½-inch round biscuit cutter, cut out as many biscuits as you can, dipping the cutter in a little flour between cuts, to prevent sticking. Make sure to lift the cutter straight up as you work, without any twisting. Arrange the biscuits on the parchment-lined sheet so they touch.

5. Gently gather the remaining dough scraps and press them into a 1-inch thick rectangle. Cut out as many biscuits as you can again, and arrange them on the sheet, snug against the others. You should now have 8 to 10 biscuits.

6. Brush the tops of the biscuits with buttermilk and bake until golden-brown, 20 to 25 minutes. While the biscuits are baking, begin to prep your sausage. Remove the biscuits from the oven when done, and brush with the melted butter.

FOR THE GOOSE BREAKFAST SAUSAGE

Two 10–11 ounce goose breasts, cubed into 1½-inch pieces

7 ounces pork fatback, cubed into 1½-inch pieces

2 teaspoons Kosher salt

½ teaspoons cayenne pepper

1 teaspoon poultry seasoning

½ teaspoon black pepper, ground

½ teaspoon garlic, granulated

½ teaspoon smoked paprika

1. Place the goose and the fatback in a metal mixing bowl, then add all of the seasonings, and toss together. Place in the freezer for 15 minutes.

2. Remove the bowl from the freezer, and begin running the goose mixture through a meat grinder, using the coarse cutting blade, allowing the mixture to drop into another mixing bowl. Once all of it is run through the machine, gently stir using a fork to rake the mix together.

3. Place a cast iron skillet over medium heat and begin portioning out the patties. Using an ice cream scooper (about 2-⅔ ounce size) scoop out on to some wax paper or parchment paper that has been lightly sprayed with a pan release spray. Dampen your hands before using them to gently press the patties into shape, making these about ½-inch thick and 3 inches in circumference. You should have about 10 patties.

4. Place the patties in the pan dry, with no oil or additional fat; the fat from the mix will be plenty to render out and keep the sausage from sticking. Cook on medium heat for 3 minutes on each side. Remove from the pan and allow it to drain on some paper towels while you continue cooking the rest. You will need to pour off the excess fat in the pan between each round that you cook.

To Serve: Once your biscuits are done, cut in half lengthwise and add a sausage patty. Top the sausage with a tablespoon or so of pepper jelly, and enjoy!

"In the bird hunter's day there is always the long walk home, during which the day's silences descend and the hunters synchronize their steps and heartbeats and turn at last to their thoughts. On good days there is always a mellow satisfaction of purpose fulfilled, implied by a warm lump of meat and feather, gristle and bone, nestled in the bag. On occasion there are those lingering visitations from the ghosts of birds missed and shots blundered, which, like most good things we lose, become increasingly plausible in hindsight. But sometimes, particularly in the face of a receding sunset or an advancing winter, a hunter, like a cowboy, can feel a bit lonesome. It's a fundament of being outdoors, in an unchecked piece of land, that we as men become small, as perhaps we were meant to be all along.

In the end that is the gift of wild birds and wild places: a reason to wander purposefully into the arms of something big and unpredictable and a little bit scary, tunneled in on the goal and not the process. Only in those afternoon moments when the birds are shot or missed and the miles spent do we turn to see how far we've come, and the tiny piece of ground we occupy, and how little our presence there actually means. It is a lonesome sort of feeling, but a piece of the frame no less, as integral as all the others, and as lovely."

—REID BRYANT
"Of Men and Dogs"
October-November 2017, *Covey Rise*

Smoked Moulard Duck with Parsnip Purée, Farro, and Citrus

CHEF JOSEPH LENN | SERVES 4-6

INGREDIENTS

2 pounds moulard duck breast
2 tablespoons whole black peppercorns
2 tablespoons whole juniper berries
½ cup Kosher salt
4 tablespoons golden cane sugar
½ teaspoon ground nutmeg
1 tablespoon ground cinnamon
Orange slices, supremed
Celery leaves, to garnish
Parsnip Purée (recipe following)
Farro (recipe following)

1. For the duck cure, grind together the peppercorns and juniper berries. Combine with remaining ingredients. Season the duck with the mixture and let sit for one day, keeping it refrigerated.

2. In a smoker heated to 180 degrees, smoke the duck for 15 to 20 minutes. Remove the duck from the smoker and let cool to room temperature.

3. Place the smoked duck on a rack under a broiler, about 1 foot from the heating source, and cook until skin is rendered and brown. Remove duck from the broiler and let it rest for 4 to 5 minutes, and then slice.

FOR THE PARSNIP PURÉE

1 tablespoon canola oil
1 pound parsnips
6 ounces vegetable broth
2 ounces heavy cream

Slice parsnips very thin, and toss with canola oil. Place the parsnips on a baking sheet and bake at 275 degrees until tender (about 30 minutes). Transfer to a blender, and purée with vegetable broth until smooth. Season with salt and pepper, and reserve, keeping warm.

FOR THE FARRO

1 cup Anson Mills Farro Piccolo
2 cups vegetable broth
Half an onion, thinly diced
1 carrot, thinly diced
1 rib celery, thinly diced
1 teaspoon salt

In a medium saucepan, combine all ingredients, and bring to a simmer over medium-high heat. Cover with a lid, and reduce heat to low and cook for 20 minutes. Reserve, keeping warm.

To Serve: Place some of the parsnip purée on the plate, then the farro, and the duck. Garnish with orange supremes and celery leaves.

"Always try recipes out once or twice before cooking for friends and family. Being familiar with the dish will help ensure a smoother dinner party."

—CHEF JOSEPH LENN

Smoked Quail Terrine

CHEF ROB MCDANIEL | SERVES TWELVE 2-OUNCE SLICES

INGREDIENTS

1½ pounds chicken breast cleaned
  and diced into large chunks
8 smoked quail breasts, deboned
4 eggs
6 ounces heavy cream
½ teaspoon pate spice
1 tablespoon Kosher salt
½ teaspoon black pepper
4 ounces minced onions
1 ounce minced black truffle
  (optional)
Dark brown sugar, for curing
Salt, for curing

1. Preheat oven to 300 degrees. Place the chicken, eggs, cream, spice, salt, and pepper in a food processor, and blend until smooth. Scrape out the chicken mixture, and place in a bowl.

2. Remove the legs and wings from the quail, leaving only the boneless breasts. (The legs are great for a snack. Simply heat on the grill or under the broiler.) Dice four of the quail breasts into ¼-inch cubes. Add this to the chicken mixture, along with the minced onion and the black truffle.

3. Test the seasoning of the chicken mixture by poaching a small amount in simmering water, then adjust the seasoning to your liking.

4. To build the terrine, fill a 2-pound terrine mold halfway with the chicken mixture; tap on the table to remove air pockets. Layer the remaining quail breasts flat on top of the chicken mixture, then cover with the remaining chicken mixture. Cover, then cook in a water bath in a 300-degree oven for 1 hour or until the internal temperature of the terrine reaches 155 degrees. Remove the terrine from the water bath, and allow to cool in the refrigerator for 24 hours.

To Serve: Once cooled, run a knife around the edge of the mold, and turn it over to release the terrine. You may have to tap it on the table to get it to release. Cut slices from the loaf, and serve cold with a small salad or an assortment of pickled vegetables, coarse ground mustard, and warm bread.

Chef's Note: For the smoked quail, I recommend a semi-boneless Manchester Farms quail cured in a mixture of equal parts dark brown sugar and salt. Cover the quail in the brown sugar and salt mixture for 4 to 5 hours, rinse, and place on a resting rack in the refrigerator to air dry overnight. Smoke in a 200-degree smoker for 30 minutes, and allow to cool.

Wild Bird Fricassee

CHEF KEVIN GILLESPIE | SERVES 4

"Hunting put food on our table my whole life, now I prefer to feed my family with things whose history I know, and I know exactly where they came from. I like the simplicity of hunting your game, processing it yourself, and serving it." —**CHEF KEVIN GILLESPIE**

INGREDIENTS

1 pound gamebird breast filets
  (any gamebird will do)
¼ cup diced bacon
1 tablespoon garlic, chopped
1 tablespoon shallots, chopped
1 tablespoon fresh sage, chopped
Juice of 1 lemon
¼ cup dry white wine
½ cup heavy cream
½ cup butter
2 tablespoons grapeseed oil
¼ cup all-purpose flour
Kosher salt, to taste
Black pepper, to taste
¼ cup chicken stock

1. Place oil and bacon in a sauté pan over medium-high heat. Cook until bacon is lightly crispy. Add half of the butter to the pan, and allow it to brown slightly.

2. Dredge breast pieces in the flour, and shake off any excess. Place these in the sauté pan, and cook until one side is golden, approximately 2 minutes.

3. Add garlic and shallots, and shake the pan to mix the contents together. Deglaze with the white wine. Add cream and stock, plus a large pinch each of salt and black pepper. Stir vigorously to combine, and add remaining butter.

4. Remove from heat, and swirl the butter into the sauce to emulsify. Add lemon juice just before serving.

Smoked Pheasant Flatbread Pizza

CHEF SEAN FINLEY | YIELDS TWO 8-INCH PIZZAS

INGREDIENTS

Smoked pheasant meat, chopped
Two 8-inch premade flatbread
    doughs
Olive oil
Salt and pepper, to taste
All-purpose Greek seasoning
Barbecue sauce of choice
    or cream cheese
Gouda cheese, shredded
Mild pepperoncini rings
Spinach leaves, fresh picked
Parmesan cheese, shredded

Chef's Note: For instructions on smoking pheasant, see page 134. You can prepare two versions of the pizza—with cream cheese as one of the sauces or barbecue sauce as the other.

1. Lightly oil and season the flatbread, leaving ¼-inch around the edge that is left bare.

2. Top each flatbread with a layer either of cream cheese or your favorite barbecue sauce and add a generous layer of chopped smoked pheasant; top this layer with shredded gouda cheese, pepperoncini, and spinach.

3. Add a little shredded Parmesan cheese to finish, and then bake at 400 degrees for 8 to 10 minutes, until all the cheese has melted and the toppings are slightly toasted.

4. Remove the flatbreads to a cutting board, slice, and serve immediately.

"My inspiration for this popular dish came from taking my staff out in Custer, South Dakota over the summer, for dinner and having a poorly made version of the dish served to me. I went back to the kitchen and quickly came up with a winner." —CHEF SEAN FINLEY

Sweet Tea Quail with Grilled Peaches and Chipotle Sorghum Bourbon Glaze

CHEF ANTHONY LAMAS | SERVES 4-6

INGREDIENTS

6 quail, dressed
1 cup sugar
¼ cup salt
1 gallon fresh tea
3 bay leaves
1 tablespoon peppercorns
Sorghum Chipotle Bourbon Glaze
   (recipe following)
Baby arugula, for serving
2 peaches, sliced
Canola oil
Salt and black pepper, to taste

1. Combine all of the ingredients except the sugar, salt, and quail in a large nonreactive pot and bring to a boil. Once boiling, add the sugar slowly to dissolve.

2. Remove and reserve 1 cup of the brine mixture for the glaze, then add the ¼ cup salt to the pot, stirring to dissolve.

3. Let cool to room temperature and then cover and refrigerate the brine for 4 to 6 hours, or until chilled. The quail and brine should be the same temperature.

4. Add the quail, cover, and refrigerate for at least 6 hours or overnight.

5. Remove quail from brine and pat dry. Brush both sides of the quail with canola oil and sprinkle with salt and black pepper.

6. Grill over charcoal for 3 minutes on each side, then brush with the bourbon glaze (save the rest for serving) and cook for another minute on each side, just until the glaze starts to caramelize.

7. Add the sliced peaches to the grill and cook just until grill marks form and the peaches begin to tenderize, about 1 minute per side.

FOR THE SORGHUM CHIPOTLE BOURBON GLAZE

1 cup of sweet tea brine
2 cups sorghum
5½ ounces chipotle chilies in
   adobo sauce
Pinch of salt
¼ cup honey
½ cup bourbon

In a small saucepan, bring the reserved 1 cup sweet tea brine to a boil, then add the sorghum, chipotle chilies, and salt. In another pan, cook off alcohol in bourbon, then cool. Add bourbon and honey to the chipotle sorghum mixture. Reduce the heat to medium high and cook until the mixture starts to thicken, about 5 minutes. Remove about a quarter of the glaze for basting the quail.

To Serve: On either a large platter or individual plates, serve the quail on a bed of baby arugula with several slices of grilled peaches. Drizzle the platter or each serving with the remaining glaze.

"Bourbon works well with gamebirds. It matches duck, quail, and pheasant, while beef is so rich you might lose the bourbon (flavor) a little bit. Gamebirds have mild flavor and bourbon adds some smoky tones, making the combo a great marriage."

—CHEF ANTHONY LAMAS

Wood-Fired Quail
CHEF GIANNI GALLUCCI | SERVES 4-6

INGREDIENTS

4 whole quail, dressed
4 ounces white wine
Salt and black pepper, to taste
2 ounces rosemary, chopped
2 ounces sage, chopped
Rainbow carrots
Heirloom potatoes
Extra-virgin olive oil
8 ounces candied cherries
4 pieces of pancetta

1. Place the deboned quail in a large bowl, and add the white wine, rosemary, and sage. Add salt and pepper to taste. Mix everything together, coating the quail well, then cover, and refrigerate overnight.

2. Lightly peel the carrots, and place on a cooking sheet with the potatoes. Drizzle extra-virgin olive oil over the vegetables and season with salt and pepper. Place in oven at 400 degrees for approximately 30 minutes. (For a wood-burning oven: cook at 700 degrees until vegetables are tender.)

3. Sear quail on each side, then remove from oven. Stuff each piece of quail with the candied cherries, then wrap each with pancetta. Place on a cooking sheet, and drizzle with extra-virgin olive oil. Cook at 350 degrees until meat is done, approximately 15 minutes.

To Serve: In a large serving dish, lay out the carrots and potatoes. Place the cooked quail on top. Add some fresh sprigs of rosemary and sage for color.

Southwestern Blue Corn Pheasant with Fruit Salsa

CHEF DENNY CORRIVEAU | SERVES 6

INGREDIENTS

6 to 8 boneless pheasant halves
Wild Cheff Lime Olive Oil
Wild Cheff Tex Mex Blend
Wild Cheff Smoky Paprika
   Chile Blend
Ground cumin, to taste
Blue corn flour, for dredging
Fruit Salsa (recipe following)

For the Fruit Salsa

½ cup papaya, diced
1 mango, diced
½ cup blueberries
4 ounces strawberries, diced
4 ounces blackberries
1 tablespoon Wild Cheff Lime
   Olive Oil
Juice of half a lime
1 teaspoon Wild Cheff Jalapeño
   Flakes
Fresh cilantro, chopped

1. Place the pheasant breasts, one at a time, into a 1-gallon Ziploc freezer bag. Using a meat mallet, gently pound them into cutlets. Remove from the bag and place onto a large dish.

2. Coat the pounded breasts on both sides with some of the Wild Cheff Lime Olive Oil, and season with the desired amount of Wild Cheff Tex Mex Blend, Wild Cheff Smoky Paprika Chile Blend, and ground cumin.

3. Place some blue corn flour in a wide bowl or into a 1-gallon Ziploc bag and dredge the breasts in it to coat. Shake off any excess.

4. Heat up a large cast iron skillet over medium-high heat, and add 2 to 3 tablespoons of olive oil and a tablespoon of butter to the pan. Once the butter melts and the pan is heated, add the breasts to the pan and cook for about 5 to 6 minutes, until both sides develop a crust created by the blue corn flour. Do not overcook the pheasant or it will become dry. The breasts are cooked when they firm up in the pan.

To Serve: Plate the cooked breasts with some fruit salsa; let the breasts rest for a couple of minutes to maintain even moisture throughout the meat before slicing them.

"Gamebird breasts can be prepared by gently pounding them with a meat mallet to make cutlets. With a cutlet, you make an even piece of meat. Anytime you cook a gamebird, think about the shape of what you're cooking. You want to create a uniform piece so it all cooks the same. You might even use a technique such as a braciole, pounding out the meat, rolling it with sauce or spices, and cooking it in the oven, or you can sauté or grill it."

—CHEF DENNY CORRIVEAU

Grouse Penne in a Morel & Parmesan Cream Sauce

CHEF DENNY CORRIVEAU | SERVES 2-4

INGREDIENTS

1½ pounds of grouse breast,
  cut into strips
Wild Cheff Lemon Olive Oil
Wild Cheff Tuscan Spice Blend
1 teaspoon of minced garlic
1 shallot, minced
1 tablespoon butter
2 tablespoons of white wine
½ cup of fresh grated Parmesan
  cheese
1 pound of penne pasta, cooked
¾ cup of Asiago cheese, shredded
  for garnish
Morel and Parmesan Cream Sauce
  (recipe following)

*For the Morel and Parmesan
Cream Sauce*

4 cups of morel mushrooms (baby
  portobello can be substituted)
1 tablespoon of butter
Wild Cheff Basil Olive Oil
2½ teaspoons of minced garlic
2 teaspoons of Wild Cheff Air-
  Dried Shallots
¼ cup of white wine (a decent
  wine you would enjoy drinking)
1½ teaspoons of apple brandy
2 cups of whipping cream
Wild Cheff French Sea Salt,
  to taste
Wild Cheff Black Pepper, to taste

1. Place strips of grouse breast meat into a bowl, and lightly coat with Wild Cheff Lemon Olive Oil and season with desired amount of Wild Cheff Tuscan or Sagebrush Spice Blend.

2. Gently sauté grouse breast pieces in a pan over medium heat (turning as you cook them), and lightly coat with more olive oil and a pat of butter. Add the garlic and shallots. Cook until meat is close to done, then remove ingredients, and set aside in a bowl.

3. For the sauce, place sauté pan back on stovetop, and bring to medium temperature setting.

4. When the pan is heated, sauté 2 cups of the morels in Wild Cheff Basil Olive Oil and butter, with garlic and shallots, while constantly stirring for approximately 5 minutes.

5. Deglaze the pan with white wine and brandy, and cook for 3 minutes longer, and then add cream. Reduce heat to low setting, and then cook sauce until thickened.

6. Add the remaining mushrooms to the sauce, along with sea salt and pepper to taste, and then the add grouse meat mixture to sauce. Stir to incorporate all ingredients, and when sauce is slightly thick, add Parmesan cheese and stir so it melts into the sauce.

To Serve: Place grouse and sauce over hot penne pasta, and sprinkle with Asiago cheese.

Buttermilk Tabasco Chicken

CHEF JOSH DRAGE | SERVES 4

INGREDIENTS

1 whole chicken (4 pieces of skin-on
  airline breast or connected leg
  and thigh)
1 pint buttermilk
5 to 10 shakes Tabasco
5 to 10 sprigs fresh thyme
1½ cups all-purpose flour
2½ cups cornmeal
Salt and pepper, to taste
2 to 4 ounces clarified butter

1. Preheat oven to 375 degrees. Trim and clean any excess fat and skin from the breast and leg/thigh.

2. Place chicken into a bowl that is good for marinating, or use a large Ziploc bag.

3. Pour buttermilk over chicken, and add the Tabasco and thyme. Make sure all ingredients are well distributed and covering all parts of the chicken. Let sit in refrigerator for at least 30 minutes and up to 2 hours.

4. Combine flour and cornmeal with salt and pepper in a large dredging bowl. Mix well.

5. Pull the chicken from the Tabasco and buttermilk, and shake off any excess. Dredge each in flour mixture, one at a time, making sure to coat it thoroughly. Shake off excess flour mixture before frying.

6. Melt clarified butter in a cast iron skillet over medium heat. Place the coated chicken, skin side down, in the heated pan, no more than 2 pieces at a time. Cook for 1 to 3 minutes until it begins to develop a nice light-brown color.

7. Place the chicken in the oven (keeping he skin side down, do not flip it over), and cook for 10 to 15 minutes, depending on chicken size and piece. (The breast will cook quicker than the thighs.) Pull the chicken from the oven, flip each piece over, and finish on medium heat, browning the underside. At this point, season liberally on one side with salt and pepper.

8. When fully cooked, pull the chicken from the heat. Season on the reverse side, and serve.

Chicken-Fried Lockhart Texas Quail on Jalapeño Creamed Corn

CHEF DEAN FEARING | SERVES 4

INGREDIENTS

4 semi-boneless quail, wings removed, birds cut in half lengthwise
3 cups all-purpose flour
6 large eggs, beaten
1 cup buttermilk
½ cup barbecue spice blend, found at specialty food markets
Salt and black pepper, to taste
2 cups vegetable oil
Jalapeño Creamed Corn (recipe following)
Cotija cheese, crumbled
Cilantro sprig, for garnish

1. For the breading station, you need three medium-sized mixing bowls. In the first mixing bowl, add half the flour. In the second mixing bowl, add the beaten eggs and buttermilk. In the third mixing bowl, combine the barbecue spice blend and the remaining flour. Mix thoroughly.

2. Prepare quail halves and dredge in the first mixing bowl of flour. Fully coat each, and shake off any excess. Dip each quail half into the second bowl of eggs and buttermilk; fully coat the quail. Dredge each quail half in the barbecue flour mixture, coating evenly. Repeat for the remaining quail halves, and set aside on a platter.

3. Place a large iron skillet over medium-high heat, and add the oil. When oil is hot, carefully place the quail skin side down in the skillet. Adjust the heat to prevent burning. Cook quail for 2 minutes, until golden brown. Turn each quail, and cook 2 more minutes. Remove onto paper towels. Season with salt and pepper.

FOR THE JALAPEÑO CREAMED CORN

1 tablespoon olive oil
1 tablespoon shallot, minced
6 ears sweet corn, shucked, cleaned, and kernels removed
1 jalapeño pepper, seeded and minced
1 cup heavy cream
Salt and black pepper, to taste
Lime juice, to taste

1. Bring a large sauté pan to medium-high heat. Add oil and shallots, sweat for 1 minute, add the corn and jalapeño into pan, and sauté for 4 minutes. Add cream, and simmer for 6 minutes or until quite thick.

2. Transfer half the corn mixture into a blender, purée on high, and fold in the remaining corn. Season with salt, pepper, and lime juice to taste.

To Serve: On four warm plates, spoon equal amounts of creamed corn in the center. Place two and a half pieces of quail atop the corn and sprinkle Cotija cheese to garnish. Add a sprig of cilantro and serve.

"The quail we serve in the restaurant comes from Lockhart, Texas, and is raised by a single farmer. I always encourage people to seek out local farms, ranches, etc…That will always lead to a great, fresh flavor profile. The bigger the quail the better, always be sure to pound the breast flat, and most importantly don't skimp on the jalapeños!"

—CHEF DEAN FEARING

Grilled Whole Chukar

CHEF CHRIS HASTINGS | SERVES 6

6 chukar, whole, bone in and skin on, with viscera removed

24 sprigs of thyme

2 ounces regular olive oil

1 tablespoon thyme, chopped

1 teaspoon fresh sage, chopped

1 teaspoon summer savory, chopped

Course salt, to taste

Course fresh ground black pepper, to taste

1. Build a wood or natural charcoal fire. Rinse and dry out cavity of birds, and season with salt and pepper. Take two sprigs of thyme per bird, crush them between your fingers to release the aroma, and place in the cavity of the birds.

2. Truss the birds with butcher's twine. Place birds in a mixing bowl with olive oil. Add thyme, sage, and summer savory, and mix evenly. Season with salt and pepper. Let marinate for one hour, at room temperature.

3. When the coals are glowing and the grill grate is hot, scrap off all excess on the grill grates with a grill brush. Wipe off excess ash with a wet towel. Drizzle oil on a towel, and use it to oil the grill.

4. Place chukar on the grill, turning often to assure all the skin is evenly golden brown and crispy, for about 10 minutes. Move birds off to the edges, back side down, and place cover on grill. Cook for 5 more minutes.

To Serve: Remove the birds from the grill onto a warm platter. Let rest for 5 minutes, and serve.

Wild Turkey Burgers

CHEF CHARLIE PALMER | YIELDS 4 LARGE BURGERS

INGREDIENTS

2 pounds ground turkey, 70
    percent lean, 30 percent fat
1 teaspoon ancho chili powder
1 teaspoon ground cumin
1 teaspoon granulated garlic
Roasted Jalapeño Guacamole
    (recipe following)
4 onion rolls

1. Combine turkey meat with ancho chili powder, ground cumin, and granulated garlic.

2. Divide turkey mix into ½-pound balls and wrap well in plastic to avoid oxidation (or turning brown on the surface). Keep the meat refrigerated until ready to grill. Remove wrap, press the meat into patties, and salt before cooking.

3. When the grill is very hot, add the patties. Cook the burgers 3 to 5 minutes per side, depending on the thickness of the burger and desired doneness. Let rest 5 minutes before serving.

FOR THE ROASTED JALAPEÑO GUACAMOLE

(yields about 3 cups)
1 large jalapeño pepper
2 limes
1 teaspoon Kosher salt
¼ cup red onion, chopped
2 avocados
¼ cup fresh cilantro, chopped

Roast a jalapeño pepper over a gas flame or on the grill. When cool enough to handle, scrape out the insides, discarding skin and seeds. Scoop out the avocado, adding this to the roasted pepper along with the lime juice, Kosher salt, chopped onion, and cilantro. Blend well.

To Serve: Serve burgers on onion rolls and top with Roasted Jalapeño Guacamole.

Chef Palmer's notes for preparing ground meat:

Using the Right Ratio: Choose a 70 percent lean cut of meat (and wild game is always leaner than pasture-raised) to 30 percent pork fat, such as fattier bacon or pork fatback. What you get from this ratio is a flavorful, moist, and juicy game burger (regardless of thickness) that will sizzle when you grill it and not just dry roast.

Grinding the Meat: When grinding meat for burger or sausage making, you need pristine equipment—your grinder must be immaculate to prevent bacteria growth.

Tools and Equipment: Freeze the grinder pieces and blades prior to use. Not only will the frigid surface temperature of the equipment inhibit bacteria, it will prevent friction from melting or "smearing" the fat (when grinding), which can hamper this vital flavor addition from becoming evenly distributed throughout the burger or sausage mix.

Grilled Wild Turkey Breast with Grilled Vegetables and Sauce Gribiche

CHEF CHRIS HASTINGS | SERVES 6

INGREDIENTS

Twelve 3-ounce wild turkey breast steaks
2 tablespoons Hastings Creations Poultry Salt or Kosher salt, divided
½ teaspoon freshly ground black pepper
1 garlic clove, crushed and peeled
¼ cup extra-virgin olive oil
Two 8-ounce heads radicchio lettuce, cut lengthwise into 6 wedges each
Two 1-pound fennel bulbs, cores trimmed and cut into 6 wedges each
6 spring Vidalia onions, cut in half lengthwise
12 jumbo asparagus stalks, bottom part trimmed, peeled, and blanched
3 to 4 tablespoons Argrumato Lemon Oil
1½ teaspoons freshly ground black pepper
1½ cups Sauce Gribiche (recipe following)

1. Toss the turkey steaks with half of the poultry salt, pepper, garlic clove, and extra-virgin olive oil in a large bowl until well seasoned. Cover the steaks and chill for 1 hour.

2. Preheat the grill to medium high (350 to 400 degrees).

3. Remove the turkey steaks from the refrigerator and allow them to continue to marinate at room temperature for 20 minutes before grilling.

4. Combine the radicchio and fennel wedges, onions, and asparagus stalks in a large bowl. Drizzle with the lemon oil, the rest of the salt, and pepper, and toss to combine.

5. Grill the vegetables on all sides, until lightly charred and tender: 1 to 2 minutes for the radicchio, 5 to 7 minutes for the fennel, 3 to 4 minutes for the onions, and 3 to 4 minutes for the asparagus. Set the vegetables aside and cover to keep warm.

6. Remove the turkey steaks from the marinade and discard the garlic clove and any excess oil. Grill the steaks for 3 to 4 minutes on each side, or until cooked through.

FOR THE SAUCE GRIBICHE

1 tablespoon Dijon mustard
¼ cup Champagne vinegar
¾ cup olive oil
1 tablespoon fresh tarragon, chopped
2 teaspoons fresh parsley, chopped
1½ teaspoons fresh chives, chopped
1½ teaspoons fresh chervil, chopped
¾ teaspoon Kosher salt
¼ teaspoon freshly ground black pepper
4 large hard-boiled eggs, peeled and grated
2 tablespoons drained capers

Whisk together the mustard and vinegar in a medium mixing bowl. While whisking constantly, slowly drizzle the oil into the mustard mixture until well combined. Stir in the tarragon, parsley, chives, and chervil and season with the salt and pepper. Fold in the grated eggs and capers and refrigerate for 30 minutes before serving. Make sure to stir the sauce again before serving.

To Serve: Arrange two pieces of the turkey steaks on each dinner plate. Place two wedges of radicchio, two wedges of fennel, one onion half, and two asparagus stalks on each plate. Spoon ¼ cup of the Sauce Gribiche over and around each plate, and serve immediately.

"When preparing wild turkey, we like to 'salt' or 'kosher' the meat by tossing it in our house-made poultry salt and marinating it for about an hour. Although it may seem like more salt than you would normally add, the end result is very flavorful. This process is not complicated and softens the slightly gamey flavor of the wild turkey meat." —CHEF CHRIS HASTINGS

Grilled Dove Breasts Wrapped in Benton's Bacon

CHEF CHRIS HASTINGS | SERVES 4

"There are three keys to perfecting this recipe. The first is to make sure your bacon is paper-thin, by allowing your butcher or favorite restaurant chef to slice slab bacon to about 1/32 of an inch. Next is to take care not to over-season the meat. Too often, dove breasts and other wild game are heavily seasoned with items such as Italian dressing or steak-sauce marinade, making it difficult to taste the pure flavor of the fresh meat. Lastly, don't over cook the dove breasts. They are best when served rare to medium-rare." —CHEF CHRIS HASTINGS

INGREDIENTS

24 dove breast halves (from 12 doves, about 14 ounces)

¾ teaspoon Kosher salt

¾ teaspoon freshly ground black pepper

12 paper-thin slices (about 3 ounces total) Benton's Bacon or other local smoked slab bacon, cut in half crosswise

2 tablespoons peanut oil, divided

Crawfish Risotto (recipe following)

1. Season the dove breast halves on both sides with the salt and pepper. Wrap each breast half in a half slice of bacon. (The bacon does not have to completely cover the breast.)

2. Heat 1 tablespoon of the peanut oil in an 8-inch cast iron skillet over medium-high heat just until the oil begins to smoke. Add half of the wrapped breasts, seam side down, and cook for 2 minutes. Turn the breasts and cook for 1 more minute (for medium-rare) or until bacon is golden and crispy on both sides.

3. Transfer to a serving plate, and keep warm until ready to serve. Add the remaining tablespoon of oil to the skillet, if needed, and preheat until just smoking. Repeat the cooking process with the remaining dove breasts.

FOR THE CRAWFISH RISOTTO WITH PRESERVED MEYER LEMONS

(yields 4 servings)

4 cups basic risotto

¼ cup finely diced leeks (white part only)

1 to 1½ cups shrimp stock

1 teaspoon Kosher salt

¼ teaspoon freshly ground black pepper

8 ounces (¾ to 1 cup) cooked crawfish tail meat

2 tablespoons diced preserved meyer lemon rind

1 tablespoon plus 1 teaspoon chopped fresh chives

1 tablespoon plus 1 teaspoon chopped fresh tarragon

1 tablespoon plus 1 teaspoon chopped fresh chervil

2 tablespoons unsalted butter

½ cup loosely packed micro greens

1. Place the risotto and leeks in a large saucepan over medium heat and stir with a wooden spoon until warmed through. Slowly add the shrimp stock, ½ cup at a time, stirring until all of the liquid is absorbed. Repeat this process, adding ½ cup after each addition is absorbed, until the rice is creamy and al dente. (You may not need all 1½ cups of stock.)

2. Season the risotto with the salt and pepper, fold in the crawfish tail meat, and cook for 1 minute or just until heated through. Remove from the heat and stir in the preserved lemon, chives, tarragon, chervil, and butter.

To Serve: Spoon about 1¼ cups of the risotto into four shallow bowls and top each with 2 tablespoons of micro greens and a dove breast. Serve immediately.

Duck Meatball Banh Mi

CHEF CHARLIE PALMER | SERVES 4-6

INGREDIENTS

1½ pounds duck thigh and breast
meat, or the meat of about 6
domestic duck legs, cut into
1-inch pieces
6 ounces fatback, cut into
¼-inch dice
Asian Spice Mix (recipe following)
6 tablespoons mayonnaise
1 tablespoon Sriracha hot
chili sauce
1 tablespoon fresh lime juice
12 fresh cilantro sprigs
1 cucumber, thinly sliced
lengthwise (about a ⅛-inch
cross-section)¼ red onion,
thinly sliced
1 jalapeño pepper, stemmed and
thinly sliced lengthwise (seeds
removed, if desired)
Four 8-inch lengths of baguette,
cut horizontally, but with a
hinged opening

For the Asian Spice Mix

½ teaspoon ground ginger
½ teaspoon dried orange peel
½ teaspoon ground cinnamon
½ teaspoon coarsely ground
black pepper
½ teaspoon ground coriander
¼ teaspoon garlic powder
¼ teaspoon ground cloves
⅛ teaspoon cayenne pepper
1 tablespoon sesame seeds
2 tablespoons soy sauce
1 tablespoon honey

1. Place the duck meat and fatback in a mixing bowl, and chill thoroughly. When the meat is sufficiently cold, add the spice mix and combine well.

2. Preheat the oven to 350 degrees and lightly grease a roasting pan. Grind the duck mixture and form 20 meatballs the size of ping-pong balls (1¼ to 1½ ounces each). Place the meatballs on the roasting pan, spacing them evenly. Roast in the oven until the meatballs are firm to the touch, with a thoroughly cooked interior and deep golden-brown exterior, about 25 to 30 minutes.

To Serve: In a small bowl, combine the mayonnaise, Sriracha, and lime juice. Set out all the vegetable ingredients for easy assembly. Open up the prepared bread segments and, using a grill or broiler, lightly toast the inside. Spread the mayonnaise mixture on the toasted side. Place the meatballs, five per sandwich, on the bottom portion of the bread. Next, layer the vegetable garnish atop the meatballs: three cilantro sprigs per sandwich, plus a few slices of cucumber to cover, and red onion and sliced jalapeño as desired. Fold the sandwich together, and press down lightly to seal.

Chef's Note: Ducks come in different sizes, and 1½ pounds of meat may mean three mallard ducks or as many as five teal ducks.

PIZZA OVEN AFIELD

Story by Addy McDaniel | Photography by Mike Schalk

Chef Gianni Gallucci brings Naples-style pizza to the South.

Gianni Gallucci has been making pizza professionally for more than 10 years, specifically Neapolitan-style pizza. Gianni, whose family is originally from Nola, a town and modern municipality in the Metropolitan City of Naples, Italy, spent his childhood days between Chicago and Italy. He recalls, "Even though I was born in the United States, I grew up going back and forth. My brother and I spent half the year in Chicago and half the year in Nola every year until we were about 16 years old." Because of Gianni's unique upbringing, he was always surrounded by the freshest ingredients and the world's best pizzaiolos.

As a kid, he would collect whatever money he could and buy a pizza to share among friends. A few years later, he realized that "It was something as simple as a pizza that could make us forget about the bad times in life and just focus on friendships." Gianni wanted to make sure that when he chose a career, he chose something of the same nature. He says, "People in Italy eat pizza almost more for a social reason than actually being hungry. In America they say, 'Hey, let's get a coffee and catch up,'

but in Naples they say, 'Hey, let's grab a pizza and talk.'"

Neapolitan pizza originated in Naples, Italy, and is made with only fresh, simple ingredients. The pizzas are generally smaller in size because they are cooked at very high temperatures—about 800 to 900 degrees—for no more than 90 seconds. Gianni began studying at a school in Naples while working alongside pizzaiolos at local pizzerias. He then attended the Academy of Pizza, a school hosted by the Associazione Pizzaiuoli Napoletani (APN), and earned his APN certification. The goal of the association is to ensure that the art of making Neapolitan pizza is passed to new generations and that the traditions are kept alive.

Now one of two APN-certified pizzaiolos in Illinois, Gianni lives with his family in Chicago. He owns a mobile catering service, Zero Ottantuno, or Zero Eighty-One (081), which is the area code for Naples. He offers a wide variety of services, from catering weddings and special events to consulting for others in the art of Neapolitan pizza making. "If I must spend the rest of my life doing one thing," Gianni declares, "watching people's reaction to my pizza and enjoyment of my dishes sounds good to me. That is much more satisfying to me than any dollar amount."

The young pizzaiolo's love for Neopolitan pies stems from his love of heritage. "My parents made a lot of

sacrifices early on to ensure that their Italian culture stayed with us," he says. "When we went on vacation we would go to Italy, not Disney World. My parents wanted to make sure that we spent as much time in Italy as possible to ensure that we didn't lose any of our heritage or traditions. They wanted to us to be able to pass it on to the next generation."

One tradition instilled in him by his upbringing—besides pizza—is his love of outdoors and upland hunting. This springs from childhood days spent afield with his father, Francesco, who passed many days in the Italian countryside with a shotgun and an English setter. He saw no reason to quit when he moved to the United States. "When my father came to this country," Gianni says, "he started hunting immediately. He landed on a Tuesday and on Thursday he was in the field."

Like father, like son: "If I get to play soccer once a week," Gianni says, "I'm happy. If I get to make pizza every day, I'm content. But from November to January, if I'm not hunting, then somebody better be sick or in the hospital!" Not only does he enjoy hunting game, he also enjoys cooking game. Growing up, Gianni recalls, they had one rule in his house: "If you shot it, you cleaned it. If you killed it, you ate it." He adds, "There are pictures of me at four years old helping my dad clean pheasants. It was just a way of life." One that he now appreciates.

Gianni decided to bring his two passions together at Roberts Shooting Preserve in Egypt, Georgia, where he

FAMILY AFFAIR

Gianni jumped at the chance to bring along his father, Francesco, to Georgia for the hunt. The pair share a deep passion for upland hunting.

QUAIL EGG PIZZA
Recipe on page 154

WOOD-FIRED QUAIL
Recipe on page 179

spent the afternoon in the field and the morning and evening creating Italian dishes full of upland game. He teamed up with Kay Heritage and Sunju Pitts of Big Bon Pizza, a mobile pizza truck in Savannah, Georgia, to create an authentic Italian feast for friends and family. Kay and Sunju brought the oven, and Gianni and his father harvested the quail. Kay and Sunju got to know Gianni a few years back when they traveled to Chicago to learn to make Naples-style pizza from him. They launched their business soon after. At the opening of Big Bon Pizza, the young chef mentioned how much he had heard about quail hunting in Georgia and asked the pair if they could get him connected to a plantation down south. Gianni said, "I will drive from Chicago just to go hunting." A couple of phone calls and one 17-hour car ride later, there he was.

Friends and family spent the evening with their taste buds enveloped in incredible flavors. Gianni prepared appetizers such as mozzarella wrapped in speck and several main dishes including paccheri Bolognese, a traditional pasta in Naples, and wood-roasted quail. They also savored pizza with roasted quail, pancetta, mozzarella, and quail eggs.

Gianni's realization of what pizza could do to bring people together proved true. Around a table filled with a bountiful harvest, no one worried about the hours spent in prep for the dinner, how much work was to be done to clean up, or how much it was going to cost. They simply enjoyed each other's company and a night reminiscing about the day's hunt. There was good music, good wine and conversation, but best of all…there was good pizza.

OUT OF THE STREAMS AND SEA

Fish & Seafood

PREPARING FISH & SEAFOOD

Tips and techniques for the new fisherman, the do-it-yourself

fishmonger, or the experienced sportsman

GRAHAM DAILEY

How do you clean and skin different types of seafood? Any tips or recommendations?

Once you figure out the anatomy of fish, even though you are preparing different species, sizes, and cuts, they all usually have the same bone structure. Always remove and clip off the fins. Two of the biggest mistakes when cleaning fish are not being careful and not taking your time. You need to make sure that you are utilizing all your tools, because they will help you. People try to go through the process too quickly, and honestly, it takes time and patience. When you fly through it, you miss out on some of the better cuts and risk hurting yourself. Make sure you take the "cheap meats" out. Another thing is you have to make sure that everything is very well iced. You don't want anything to spoil before you have time to cook it.

How do you peel and devein shrimp?

My style is different than most. A lot of people will peel the shrimp first, remove the head, take the legs off, and then remove the shell. When I was in France, I picked up a new technique. I take a very small paring knife, turn it upside down, hold it onto the blade and remove the head of the shrimp. Then I invert the blade of the knife into the spine of the shrimp and run it all the way down to the tail. You can peel the entire shrimp at once, and it speeds up the process. It also takes out the vein in the spine all at once, so you are not doing multiple steps. This allows you to

avoid touching the shrimp over and over. Pick it up, peel it, and you're done. Once I picked up this trick, I kept saying to myself: "Why have I been doing it the other way for so long?"

What do you recommend to fishermen on being creative on how they cook different types of fish and seafood?

I like to keep things simple. I am a big believer in letting the fish flavors speak for themselves. I do not like to use a lot of herbs and spices. As I have matured as a chef, I have gone back to simplicity. I do a lot of cooking with the skin on. You want to taste things for what they really are. Stone crab claws are one of those perfect foods. They don't need a whole lot, just some salt, pepper, and a little bit of lemon juice, and they are fantastic. Other fish and shellfish are all the same way. You don't need a lot of extras. Different types of snapper taste different, depending on what they are eating and the environment they are living in. In my cooking, I cook a lot with cast iron pans, or outside grills, and just salt, pepper, and a little bit of lemon juice. I want to be able to taste those rich, natural flavors.

What's the go to way to prepare a whole fish and fillets for eating?

When I cook a whole fish, I like to do what people call "on the half shell." For this you leave the skin on.

It's mostly used with fish that are bigger and harder to fillet and remove the skin. I just put them right on the grill or in the cast iron pan. When I fillet a fish, it tends to be a much smaller fish. I use salt, pepper, olive oil, and finish it with a pat of butter and a little bit of lemon juice.

How do you prepare and fillet a fish?

If I'm out fishing and I catch one I want to keep, I will go ahead and gut it and put it on ice. You start out by removing the pectoral fins. Be careful because those will spine you. They are very sharp, and some of them are poisonous. They also carry a lot of bacteria, so be careful when doing this. Then I descale. I then take out the fillets, starting with the top of the head and working my way down the spine and fillet. Most of the time I keep the skin on the fish until I cook it. When I'm scaling larger whole fish, I use a garbage bag and put the fish inside it and scale it inside the garbage bag. You will not get scales all over your workstation, and it makes for an easy cleanup.

When do you keep the skin on or off the fish and seafood?

I normally keep the skin on fish and seafood as much as possible, if it is viable. A lot of fish, especially coldwater fish, have a beautiful fat layer between the skin and the flesh. It's like good marbling on a steak. You don't want to remove it if it adds to the natural flavor profile. But a lot of people don't like fish with the skin on, so normally what I do is cook it with the skin on and wait until the last moment, then remove it before serving. There are some fish that you don't want to cook with the skin on. It depends on whether they have a slimy texture, or the skin is unappealing visually. Others are not edible at all. These fish tend to be the ones without scales. Swordfish and tuna, for example: No matter what you do, the skin is just like leather.

How much time do you have, in certain conditions, from taking the fish from the water to icebox, and eventually preparation and eating?

It's different for every condition. It's important to be aware of where you are and how hot it is. Ice and cool temperatures are going to be your friends. When I catch a fish, I immediately put it on ice. When I prepare fish, I use cool surfaces, in a cool room. I know that is not feasible for everyone, so the main thing is being flexible and conscious and keeping the fish as cold as possible, moving it as quickly as possible.

What type utensils and knives do you need when preparing?

I use different types of tools for different types of fish. For larger fish, I always use tin snips. I keep them in my toolbox, and they always come in handy. They cut through large dorsal and pectoral fins. On smaller fish, I use a set of general shears. Removing tails and fins with a knife is very difficult. I use a long slicer, tweezers, and a paring knife for small detail work on fish. I also always have a flexible knife handy. When you are working with fish, you need to be able to adjust to all its bumps and ridges. I use a spoon to remove the meat inside of bones and on the rib cages. I have a stronger, heavier French knife to use when cracking bones and removing heads. It's important to have one for your more aggressive work.

What are the best surfaces to prepare fish and seafood?

I always cut on a rubber or plastic cutting board, and I like it to be big. It doesn't make sense to prepare a big fish on a small cutting board. That's how you injure yourself, and you lose out on some of the meat on the fish. Give yourself plenty of workspace and have a large cutting board that is very sturdy and doesn't move. Also, you want to keep the fish as close to you as you can so you have more control over it and the knife.

How long does fish last if frozen?

I never freeze my fish. I like to use common conservation practices like catch-and-release. I'm big on sustainable seafood. If I'm not going to eat it, I put it back. If the fish is a nice size and I know it will feed my family, I will take it. I think you can tell when a fish has been frozen. It becomes very mealy. I believe that eating fresh fish is the best practice, and it will change the way you eat. 🐟

Aquavit Smoked Trout

CHEF JOSH DRAGE | SERVES 1-2

INGREDIENTS

6 rainbow trout fillets
1 cup Kosher salt
⅓ cup sugar
Zest of 3 blood oranges
10 to 12 juniper berries
2 ounces Aquavit

1. Combine salt, sugar, orange zest, juniper, and aquavit. Rub the brine on both sides of the trout, and place neatly in a large Ziploc bag.

2. Let marinate for one hour. Pull trout from bag, and rinse off brine under running water. Place trout skin side down on a rack to dry. Keep refrigerated.

3. Remove the trout and smoke at 175 degrees until lightly cooked, about 30 minutes. Bring the heat up if needed, to finish cooking.

Crab-Stuffed Portobello Caps

CHEF SEAN FINLEY | SERVES 4

INGREDIENTS

4 portobello mushrooms, full cap
1 pound jumbo lump crab meat
Olive oil
Fresh-chopped garlic
Fresh thyme, chopped
Rosemary
Kosher salt
Black pepper
1½ cups shredded mozzarella
   cheese
1½ cups cream cheese
1 cup shredded Parmesan cheese
3 tablespoons Old Bay Seasoning

1. Remove the stems from each portobello cap and wipe off any dirt with a damp paper towel. Place the mushrooms into a large bowl or pan and coat them with enough olive oil, fresh-chopped garlic, chopped thyme, rosemary, Kosher salt, and pepper to marinate. Let stand while you prepare the crab stuffing.

2. In a large mixing bowl, combine the lump crab meat, mozzarella cheese, cream cheese, and 2 tablespoons of the Old Bay seasoning. Using your hands, knead the ingredients thoroughly together.

3. Fill each portobello cap with a generous portion of the crab stuffing. Repeat for as many portobello caps as you have. Place the stuffed mushrooms onto a sheet pan lined with parchment paper. Sprinkle Parmesan cheese and more Old Bay seasoning over the tops of each mushroom.

4. Bake at 400 degrees for 20 minutes until the mushrooms are cooked and the stuffing is bubbly and browned on top.

To Serve: Place the mushrooms on a board and cut into wedges.

Pan-Seared Soft Shell Crab BLT with Arugula and Roasted Tomato Butter

CHEF GRAHAM DAILEY | SERVES 4

INGREDIENTS

4 soft-shell crabs
½ cup cornmeal
½ cup corn flour
2 tablespoons canola oil
2 tablespoons unsalted butter
2 cups arugula
2 tablespoons Roasted Tomato
    Vinaigrette (recipe page 234)
4 slices white bread, toasted
1 cup crème fraîche
8 slices bacon, cooked
Basil Oil, for garnish (recipe
    following)
Roasted Tomato Butter, for
    garnish (recipe following)
Kosher salt and black pepper

1. Use kitchen shears to clean the crabs. For each crab: cut half inch off the front, including the eyes and mouth. Find the sack in the gut and remove its contents. Lift one corner of the crab's shell to access and remove the gills; repeat on the other side. Flip the crab over, and cut off the belly flap. Lightly rinse the cleaned crab in cool water, and pat dry with a kitchen towel.

2. In a shallow dish, combine the cornmeal, corn flour, and ½ teaspoon each of salt and pepper. Dredge the clean crabs in this breading mixture, and shake off any excess.

3. In a large saucepan, heat the oil and butter over medium-high heat. When the oil is hot, add the crabs to the pan topside down. (There should be space between each crab; if not, cook them in batches.)

Cook, turning once, about 1 to 3 minutes per side, until golden brown. Remove the cooked crabs from the oil, and drain on a plate lined with paper towels.

FOR THE BASIL OIL

(yields 2 cups)
4 cups water
2 ounces basil leaves
2 cups olive oil
Kosher salt

1. In a large saucepan, bring the water to a boil over medium-high heat. Add the basil, and cook until bright green, about 10 to 20 seconds. Transfer immediately to a bowl of ice water to stop the cooking process, and leave for one minute, then drain and pat dry with a kitchen towel.

2. In a blender, combine the basil and oil, and purée until smooth. Pour the oil into a large, fine-mesh strainer lined with several layers of cheesecloth, and slowly strain into a bowl.

*FOR THE ROASTED
TOMATO BUTTER*

3 large tomatoes, quartered
1 tablespoon olive oil
Kosher salt and black pepper
2 cups white wine
1 cup heavy cream
4 sticks unsalted butter, room
    temperature

1. Preheat the oven to 400 degrees. Place the tomatoes on a sheet pan, drizzle with olive oil, and season

lightly with salt and pepper. Roast until slightly charred, for 20 to 25 minutes.

2. Remove from the oven. In a medium saucepan, combine the roasted tomatoes and the wine, and bring to a simmer over medium heat. Cook until the liquid reduces by half, about 6 to 8 minutes.

3. Add the heavy cream, and simmer until reduced by half again, another 6 to 8 minutes. Remove from the heat, and in a mixer, blend until smooth. Return the sauce to the pan, warm over low heat, and slowly whisk in the butter until sauce is emulsified. Remove from the heat, and season with salt and pepper, to taste.

To Serve: Toss the arugula with the vinaigrette. Toast the bread. Cook the bacon, and drain. Place a small dollop of crème fraîche on each of four plates and top with the toast. Cut each slice of bacon into three sections and place across toast. Top with the dressed arugula and soft-shell crab. Garnish with Basil Oil and Roasted Tomato Butter, and season with salt and pepper, to taste.

Pan-Seared Nantucket Bay Scallops with Roasted Cauliflower and Prosciutto

CHEF GRAHAM DAILEY | SERVES 4

INGREDIENTS

40 Nantucket bay scallops (about ½ pound)
5 tablespoons olive oil, divided
½ teaspoon Kosher salt, plus more for seasoning
½ teaspoon white pepper, plus more for seasoning
½ head cauliflower, cut into large florets and halved lengthwise
1 tablespoon unsalted butter
2 tablespoons panko breadcrumbs
1 teaspoon minced chives
8 very thin slices prosciutto (or cured country ham)
4 tablespoons Roasted Lemon Vinaigrette (recipe following)

1. Preheat the oven to 350 degrees.

2. Add 3 tablespoons of the olive oil to an oven-safe, large, nonstick skillet. Sprinkle the salt and pepper over the oil, and swirl to coat the bottom of the pan. Evenly arrange the cauliflower cut side down in the skillet, and place the skillet over medium heat. Leave the cauliflower alone to brown, about 4 to 6 minutes. Then move the skillet to the oven, and cook the cauliflower for 10 to 15 minutes, until it begins to brown on top.

3. Return the pan to the stovetop over medium heat, and stir in the butter. Sprinkle the breadcrumbs over the cauliflower, and toss to combine. Cook until the breadcrumbs brown slightly, 1 to 2 minutes. Stir in the chives, and season with salt and pepper, to taste. Set aside.

4. Season the scallops very lightly with salt and pepper. In a large nonstick skillet, heat the remaining oil over medium-high heat. Working in batches, add the scallops, and leave them alone to sear for 2 minutes. Sauté the scallops until slightly cooked, about 1 minute more.

FOR THE ROASTED LEMON VINAIGRETTE
(yields 2 cups)
2 lemons, halved
¼ cup champagne vinegar
1 tablespoon minced shallot
¼ cup minced garlic
1½ cups olive oil
Kosher salt and black pepper

1. Preheat the grill to high. Place the lemons on the grill, cut side down, and cook until lightly charred, 4 to 6 minutes. Then remove the lemons from the grill with tongs, cool, and juice.

2. In a medium bowl, combine ¼ cup of the lemon juice, vinegar, shallot, and garlic, and set aside for 10 minutes. (This will mellow the flavor of the shallot and garlic.) Add the olive oil in a thin stream, whisking constantly, until the vinaigrette emulsifies. Season with salt and pepper to taste.

To Serve: Divide the cauliflower, scallops, and prosciutto among four plates. Drizzle with the lemon vinaigrette.

Barbecue Shrimp Taco with Mango Pickled Red Onion Salad

CHEF DEAN FEARING | YIELDS 4 TACOS

INGREDIENTS

1 cup shrimp, peeled, deveined, and diced
½ tablespoon vegetable oil
Salt, to taste
Freshly cracked black pepper, to taste
1 cup onions, diced
1 cup barbecue sauce
½ cup jalapeño jack cheese, grated
Four 6-inch flour tortillas, cooked and warm
Mango Pickled Red Onion Salad (recipe following)
⅓ cup grated Cotija cheese or Mexican farmer's cheese
⅓ cup toasted and coarsely ground Mexican pumpkin seeds
4 fresh serrano chilies
4 sprigs fresh cilantro

1. Place oil in a large sauté pan over medium heat. Add shrimp to hot pan, season with salt and pepper, and sauté for 1 minute until the shrimp turn red. Add onions, and sauté for 2 minutes or until translucent.

2. Stir in barbecue sauce, bring to a boil, and quickly remove pan from heat. Add cheese, and stir to combine until cheese has melted into mixture.

FOR THE MANGO PICKLED RED ONION SALAD

1 red onion
½ cup white wine vinegar
½ cup white sugar
2 ripe mangos, peeled and cut into thin julienne
3 cups green cabbage, rib removed, julienned
½ cup pecans, toasted
¼ cup cilantro, finely sliced
Smoky Cumin Lime Vinaigrette (recipe following)
Salt, to taste

1. Peel onion. Cut in half and slice into very thin half-moon shapes. Put in a small bowl and set aside.

2. Heat vinegar and sugar (50/50 mix) in a small saucepan over medium heat, stirring constantly. When sugar dissolves, remove from heat. Add a pinch of salt and pour over onion in container, then cover with plastic. Put it in the refrigerator and allow to stand overnight to pickle, approximately 8 to 12 hours. When cool, use strainer to drain pickling mixture from onions and use for the salad.

3. Place the remaining ingredients and pickled red onion into a medium bowl, and slowly add vinaigrette until salad is lightly coated. Season with salt, and serve immediately.

FOR THE SMOKY CUMIN LIME VINAIGRETTE

½ cup olive oil
½ cup vegetable oil
½ cup fresh lime juice
1 small onion, diced and cold-smoked for 20 minutes
1 cup fresh orange juice
½ tablespoon whole cumin, toasted
2 tablespoons malt vinegar
3 tablespoons maple syrup
Salt, to taste

1. Combine the oils and lime juice in a medium-size bowl. Reserve.

2. Add smoked onions, orange juice, cumin, vinegar, and maple syrup to a small sauce pot, and bring to a boil. Cook until mixture has reduced to almost dry, about 5 minutes. Place smoked onion mixture into blender, and purée until smooth.

3. Add the purée to the oil and lime juice mixture in the medium bowl. Season with salt, and stir until completely blended.

To Serve: Place a warm tortilla in the middle of each warm serving plate. Spoon equal portions of the prepared shrimp mixture into the middle of each tortilla. Roll each tortilla into a cylinder with the seam side down. Add a small portion of Mango Pickled Red Onion Salad on top of each taco. Sprinkle each with Cotija cheese and Mexican pumpkin seeds and garnish with fresh serrano chilies (the adventurous can eat these like pickles) and sprigs of cilantro.

Brown Sugar & Bourbon-Cured Smoked Salmon

CHEF CHARLIE PALMER | SERVES 4-8

"When you're cooking for the outdoors, versatility is a priority. With weather changes come activity shifts, and it's always a good idea to invest your time in recipes with flexibility. Once cured and smoked, you can serve this salmon on pumpernickel rolls with pickled cucumber, red onion, and jalapeños, or with mustard and dill yogurt. It's a natural with eggs, or you can really show off by making kedgeree, a cross-cultural Anglo-Indian dish that's become a traditional British brunch favorite, and that is nourishing but a touch elegant." —**CHEF CHARLIE PALMER**

INGREDIENTS

Four 10-ounce salmon steaks or
   salmon fillets, scaled
1 cup firmly packed dark
   brown sugar
1 cup Kosher salt
¼ teaspoon cayenne pepper
¼ cup bourbon

1. Prepare hardwood chips for smoking; cherry gives a nice flavor finish.

2. Mix together the brown sugar, salt, and cayenne, then incorporate the bourbon. Scatter half the cure mixture into a flat container or tray with tall sides, that is also large enough to hold all of the salmon steaks in a single layer. Place in steaks, and pour the remaining cure mixture over the top of the salmon, spreading it over the entire surface of the fish.

3. Cover the container with plastic wrap and refrigerate the fish for up to 12 hours, flipping each portion of fish two or three times throughout the curing process. As water and natural juices are pulled from the fish, they will mix with the cure solution to create a brine. When cured, the salmon flesh will be firmer, with a deep golden-orange color. Rinse the fish completely in cool water to remove excess salt, and pat dry with paper towels.

4. Place the fish on a baking rack set over a baking sheet, return to the refrigerator, and let the surface dry for 4 to 6 hours. During this time, a pellicle, or a sticky/tacky layer, will form on the outside of the fish. This allows the smoke to stick to the fish with maximum effect. If the surface of the fish is too wet, the smoke will not adhere properly, and the acidic layer that smoke provides for preservation will not take evenly.

5. Place the fish on a lightly oiled rack on (or in) a smoker outfitted with hardwood chips. Follow the instructions on the smoker for the smoking of fish. Portions of fish will take 40 to 50 minutes to smoke well and cook through.

Bayou La Batre Shrimp and Conecuh County Sausage Gumbo

CHEF CHRIS HASTINGS | SERVES 10-12

INGREDIENTS

1 cup peanut oil

1¼ cups all-purpose flour

3 cups diced onion

1 cup diced celery

1 cup seeded and diced red
   bell pepper

1 cup seeded and diced
   poblano pepper

2 tablespoons minced garlic

2 bay leaves

2 teaspoons fresh thyme leaves

One 12-ounce bottle light beer

7 cups Chicken Stock (recipe
   following)

2 pounds peeled 21/25 shrimp

1 tablespoon plus 1 teaspoon salt

2 teaspoons freshly ground
   black pepper

1 teaspoon cayenne pepper

1 pound Conecuh brand smoked
   sausage or other spicy smoked
   sausage, such as Andouille

¾ pound sliced okra (fresh or
   frozen and thawed)

2 cups seeded and diced tomatoes

1 cup chopped green onion tops

4 to 5 cups cooked rice, for serving

1. Heat the oil in a large, heavy-bottomed (preferably cast iron) skillet over medium heat. Whisk in the flour and cook, stirring constantly, until the mixture darkens to a rich, reddish-brown color, 30 to 35 minutes. (Be careful not to let the flour burn or the gumbo will taste burned.)

2. Once the roux reaches the desired color, add the onion, celery, and peppers and cook, stirring, for 2 to 3 minutes. Add the garlic, bay leaves, and thyme and cook an additional 1 to 2 minutes. Whisk in the beer, stirring to scrape any browned bits on the bottom of the skillet.

3. Transfer the roux mixture to a large Dutch oven or stockpot, over medium-high heat. Add the chicken stock, salt, pepper, and cayenne pepper and bring the mixture to a boil. Reduce the heat, and simmer the gumbo for 20 minutes, stirring occasionally.

4. While the gumbo is simmering, slice the sausage lengthwise and then make crosswise cuts, forming ½-inch thick half-moons. Place the sausage in a large skillet over medium heat and cook, stirring occasionally, until the sausage is rendered and lightly browned, 8 to 10 minutes. Transfer the sausage to a paper towel-lined plate and pat dry.

5. Add the cooked sausage, okra, and tomatoes to the gumbo and simmer an additional 30 minutes, stirring occasionally. Adjust the seasonings to taste, adding more salt or pepper, if needed. Stir in shrimp for the last two minutes of simmer. Just before serving, remove and discard the bay leaves and stir in the green onions.

To Serve: Ladle the gumbo into warmed soup bowls and top with cooked rice. Serve hot.

"Conecuh is a county in South Alabama. The Conecuh Sausage Company is a small, family-owned operation that has been making well-seasoned sausages and cured meats since 1947 in the small town of Evergreen. This is our tribute to their wonderful products and it is has been the perfect accompaniment to our staff crawfish boil every January. There are many types of gumbo, but we prefer those that start with a medium-dark roux. To achieve the perfect depth of flavor, the color of the roux must match the retro reddish-brown tiles on the floor in our kitchen. If you like your gumbo spicy, try the Cajun-smoked or Spicy and Hot Hickory-Smoked styles of Conecuh sausage." —**CHEF CHRIS HASTINGS**

(yields 5 quarts)

One 5-pound whole chicken or
  3 to 4 pounds chicken bones
3 medium onions, peeled and
  roughly chopped, about 8 cups
4 large carrots, peeled and roughly
  chopped, about 2 cups
4 celery stalks, peeled and roughly
  chopped, about 2 cups
2 large garlic cloves, smashed and
  peeled
6 fresh thyme sprigs
1 bay leaf
1 tablespoon Kosher salt
5 quarts cold water

Chef's Note: We like to prepare the stocks we make at home using the whole chicken method. It gives the stock a richer flavor and yields tender cooked chicken for use in other dishes. At the restaurant, we generally use the chicken bone method.

If using a whole chicken: Rinse the chicken under cold running water and pat dry. Place the chicken in a large stockpot or Dutch oven and add the remaining ingredients. Bring the mixture to a boil, reduce the heat to low and simmer for 45 to 50 minutes, skimming off any foam that rises to the top. Remove the whole chicken from the water mixture and set aside to cool slightly. Continue to simmer the broth mixture for an additional 30 minutes, skimming occasionally. Strain the broth through fine-mesh sieve or strainer and discard the solids. The stock can be used immediately, or chilled and kept refrigerated for up to three days, or frozen for up to one month. The meat can be pulled off of the whole chicken and reserved for another use.

If using chicken bones: Rinse the bones under cold running water and drain. Place the bones in a large stockpot or Dutch oven and add the remaining ingredients. Bring the mixture to a boil, reduce the heat to low, and simmer for 1 hour, skimming off any foam that rises to the top. Strain the broth through a fine-mesh sieve or strainer and discard the bones and vegetables. The stock can be used immediately, or chilled and kept refrigerated for up to three days, or frozen for up to one month.

"So many of us fish because we appreciate the fight and the direct sensory line we are able to create between ourselves and a creature that is fundamentally wild. There is something endlessly compelling about that relationship. But in so much of the world, that relationship takes on a different level of connection. On a recent trip to the Brazilian Amazon, I spent several weeks exploring sport-fishing opportunities in the company of indigenous hunters and anglers. For those folks, the idea of fishing purely for recreation was inconceivable. Fish, and the river ecosystem that supported them, provided nourishment, plain and simple. We ate what we caught, and though there were obvious preferences, nothing was wasted. In fishing for food, I came to see something quite special in a relationship based on necessity. In some ways, without ever having needed to fish before, I'd been unable to fully appreciate the full depth and breadth of being an angler, and identifying as one."

—BRIAN GROSSENBACHER
Photographer and Outdoorsman

Fresh Trout with Horseradish and Lemon Zest

CHEF JOSH DRAGE | SERVES 1-2

INGREDIENTS

1 trout, filleted and boned, skin on
Zest of one lemon
1 tablespoon fresh horseradish
2 tablespoons olive oil
Sea salt, to taste
Fresh cracked black pepper
Chili flakes, to taste
Clarified butter

1. Combine the lemon zest, horseradish, olive oil, salt, pepper, and chili flakes, and mix together with the trout fillets in a Ziploc bag.

2. Remove the fillets from the Ziploc and lay them skin side down on a baking sheet. Spoon the remaining lemon zest-horseradish mixture over the fillets and rub this in, on the flesh side only. Let sit for 30 minutes in a refrigerator.

3. Heat a cast iron pan to medium heat, and add in clarified butter.

4. Place each fillet flesh side down in the heated pan. Lightly sear for 1 to 2 minutes, to get a touch of color, then flip them over and cook another 2 minutes, skin side down. When almost done, remove the fillets and lay them flesh side down on a clean food surface. The fillets will finish cooking outside the pan.

To Serve: Plate the fillets immediately when done: Peel off the skin, flip each fillet over so they are flesh side up, and serve.

Shrimp & Smoked Cheddar Chipotle Sweet Corn Grit Cakes with Chipotle Bourbon Orange Glaze

CHEF ANTHONY LAMAS | SERVES 4-6

INGREDIENTS

3 pounds Kentucky freshwater shrimp (U-10), peeled, washed, and deveined (You may substitute large USA wild-caught shrimp)
1 lemon, squeezed
1 tablespoon fresh chopped garlic
1 teaspoon ground oregano
1 teaspoon ground white pepper
1 teaspoon crushed red pepper
1 tablespoon Kosher salt
¼ cup olive oil
Smoked Cheddar Chipotle Sweet Corn Grit Cakes (recipe following)
Chipotle Bourbon Orange Glaze (recipe following)

1. Whisk ingredients together in bowl, then add the shrimp, tossing with the marinade to coat. Cover and refrigerate for 2 to 4 hours.

2. Grill marinated shrimp for 2½ to 3 minutes on each side.

FOR THE GRIT CAKES

3 quarts of water
¼ cup olive oil
1 teaspoon Kosher salt
3-quart container of quick grits
One 6-ounce can of chipotle chilies in adobo sauce
2 pounds of smoked cheddar cheese cut into 1-inch pieces
1¼ cup of fresh raw Silver Queen Corn, cut off cobs (about 4 cobs)
½ pound unsalted butter
¼ cup flour

1. Bring water, olive oil, and salt to a boil in large pot. Add grits slowly, about ¼ cup at a time, continually whisking. As grits begin to thicken, add butter and chilies. Cook for about 2 minutes, and lower heat. Slowly add cheese, and stir. Stir in corn, and remove from heat.

2. Using a paper towel, generously grease a sheet pan with olive oil. Pour the grit mixture into the sheet pan using a rubber spatula and spread evenly. Cover with plastic wrap and refrigerate for 4 to 6 hours, or up to 24 hours. The mixture will coagulate.

3. When thoroughly chilled, use a cookie cutter to cut the grits into the desired shape to create mini grit cakes, or cut into small triangles using a butter knife. Dust each shaped grit cake with flour and pan fry in olive oil for about 2 minutes on each side, until slightly golden. Place the fried grit cakes on a cooking sheet and finish in oven at 350 degrees for 3 to 5 minutes.

FOR THE GLAZE

¼ cup Woodford Reserve bourbon
1 onion, chopped
1 tablespoon garlic, chopped
3 ounces chipotle in adobo sauce
1 cup crushed tomatoes
1 cup ketchup
½ cup rice wine vinegar
¼ cup Worcestershire sauce
1 cup thawed frozen orange juice concentrate
¼ cup honey
1 tablespoon paprika
1 tablespoon chili powder
1 teaspoon salt

Combine ingredients together into a bowl. Refrigerate until ready for use.

To Serve: Place a grit cake in the center of each plate and spoon glaze around the grit cake. Place three grilled shrimp on each plate, surrounding the grit cake, with tails toward the center.

Tuna Old Fashioned

CHEF ANTHONY LAMAS | SERVES 4-6

INGREDIENTS

1 pound sushi-grade tuna
¼ cup bluegrass soy sauce
Juice of 3 limes
Juice of 1 orange
1 teaspoon fresh ginger, chopped
¼ cup bourbon
1 teaspoon sambal chili
1 teaspoon sesame oil
Pineapple Salsa (recipe following)

For the Pineapple Salsa

1 cup diced pineapple
½ cup diced tomato
Juice of 1 lime
2 tablespoons cilantro
1 teaspoon sesame oil
1 teaspoon soy
1 jalapeño, diced

1. Dice tuna into ⅛- to ¼-inch squares and refrigerate until ready to serve.

2. Whisk soy sauce, lime juice, orange juice, chili, and sesame oil together in a small bowl to create your broth and set aside. Refrigerate for up to 6 hours.

3. For the pineapple salsa, combine all the ingredients, except for the cilantro, and mix well. Cover and refrigerate until ready to serve the ceviche.

To Serve: Have ready six highball or rocks glasses. Place about 4 ounces of tuna in the bottom of each glass. Pour approximately 1 ounce of broth over the tuna (evenly portion among the glasses). Stir the cilantro into the salsa, then place 2 tablespoons salsa on top of the tuna. Place an orange twist on the edge of each glass, then sprinkle on micro greens or celery leaves and a thin slice of radish for bite.

"As far as I'm concerned, bourbon is its own food group. But you don't want raw alcohol flavor, you want a hint. I'll introduce bourbon to grits, apple bread pudding, macadamia ice cream, mint pesto lamb, shrimp with bourbon orange glaze, pineapple, ginger, sesame soy broth..."

—CHEF ANTHONY LAMAS

Seared Scallops with White Cheddar Grits, Sweet Corn Chowder, and Pulled Barbecue Pork Tenderloin

CHEF KIPP BOURDEAU | SERVES 4

FOR THE SCALLOPS

8 fresh scallops, U-10 size
1 teaspoon olive oil

1. Remove side muscle from scallops, pat dry with a paper towel, and season each scallop with sea salt.

2. Place a nonstick sauté pan over medium heat, add olive oil, and place scallops in pan. Let scallops sear for about 5 minutes on each side until golden brown, then remove from pan. Keep warm.

FOR THE GRITS

1 cup Anson Mills
   stone-ground grits
4 cups chicken stock
1 cup white cheddar cheese, grated
1 tablespoon herb Boursin cheese
White pepper and sea salt, to taste

In a medium saucepan over medium heat bring chicken stock to low simmer; slowly add grits, whisking to avoid lumps. Let simmer for 15 to 20 minutes until smooth and creamy, stirring occasionally. Adjust thickness with chicken stock if needed. Stir in cheeses, and season with white pepper and sea salt. Keep warm.

FOR THE CHOWDER

2 strips applewood smoked
   bacon, diced
1 white onion, small dice
1 celery rib, small dice
4 ears sweet corn, removed
   from cobb
4 cups chicken stock
2 tablespoons cornstarch, dissolved
   with 2 tablespoons of chicken
   stock or water
1 Idaho potato, peeled and diced

1. In a large stockpot over medium heat add bacon, cooking this until lightly browned, about 4 to 5 minutes. Add the onion, celery, and sweet corn, and cook for 4 to 5 minutes.

2. Add the chicken stock, and stir this through, then bring to a low simmer and cook for 10 to 15 minutes. Dissolve the cornstarch in 2 tablespoons of chicken stock or water to form a slurry, then add this to the stockpot, stirring it throughly. Cook for another 5 minutes.

3. Remove the chowder to a blender, and purée until smooth. Return the puréed chowder to the stockpot on medium heat. Add the potatoes and cook until tender, about 10 minutes. Keep warm on stovetop.

FOR THE PULLED BARBECUE PORK TENDERLOIN

1 pork tenderloin, trimmed
Coarse ground pepper, to taste
Sea salt, to taste
1 teaspoon olive oil
½ sweet onion, sliced thin
½ Granny Smith apple, peeled,
   sliced thin
1 teaspoon fresh thyme
1 cup chicken stock
½ cup barbecue sauce

1. Season pork with sea salt and coarse ground pepper. Place a large sauté pan over high heat and add olive oil. In the same pan, sear the pork on all sides until golden brown. Remove from pan, and set aside.

2. To the pan, add the onion, sliced apple, and the fresh thyme; cook for 3 to 5 minutes. Deglaze pan with chicken stock (scraping the brown bits from bottom of the pan; they add flavor). Then add the barbecue sauce and stir this through, mixing well. Return pork to pan, reduce heat to low, cover with lid and let simmer for 30 to 45 minutes until pork becomes very tender.

3. Remove pork from pan to a cutting board or platter and shred the meat, using a pair of forks positioned back to back and pulling these apart from each other as you work along. When done, return the shredded (or "pulled") meat to the pan, stirring this into the prepared sauce to coat. Let simmer another 10 minutes, then keep it warm on the stovetop.

To Serve: Warm four pasta-style serving bowls in oven and remove when ready. Divide the corn chowder between the bowls. Spoon about 3 ounces of the grits in center of each bowl. Place 2 ounces of pulled pork in the center of grits, and arrange two scallops over the pork. Garnish with herbs, and serve immediately.

Smoked Fish Potato Cake

CHEF JOSH DRAGE | SERVES 1-2

INGREDIENTS

4 ounces smoked sturgeon
6 small red new potatoes
1 bunch fresh parsley
2 tablespoons mayonnaise
Zest of one lemon
2 eggs
Sea salt, to taste
Black pepper, to taste
Red chili flakes, to taste
Clarified butter
One small bunch of chives
Fresh radish, for serving
Arugula, for serving

1. Cook the potatoes in water until cooked through, drain, then chill.

2. Pick the leaves from the parsley stems and give the leaves a good rough chop, then add to a large mixing bowl. Zest the lemon into the same bowl and add the mayonnaise.

3. Add the chilled potatoes to the bowl, breaking them apart by hand into small pieces. Do not mush it up.

4. Add the eggs, salt, pepper, and chili flakes to the mixing bowl, and blend everything together thoroughly.

5. Pick apart the smoked fish, and fold this into the potato mixture.

6. Heat a cast iron pan to medium heat, and add in clarified butter.

7. Using a tablespoon, place large rounded scoops of the fish and potato mixture in the pan, using an offset spatula to slightly flatten them to about an inch thick.

8. Sear the cakes slowly on one side until golden brown, then flip over and sear on the other side, cooking about 8 to 10 minutes total. Turn the heat down slightly, as needed, to sear and cook them through at the same time, without burning.

To Serve: Sprinkle with freshly cut chives on the Potato Cake. Serve with a remoulade sauce, fresh radish, and arugula if you like. If feeling opulent, add a large scoop of sturgeon caviar as garnish.

Trout in Foil with Lemon-Sage Butter

CHEF CHARLIE PALMER | SERVES 4

INGREDIENTS

4 whole trout, 10 to 12 ounces each, gutted and scaled

8 tablespoons (1 stick) Lemon-Sage Butter (recipe following)

1. Rinse the cavities of the fish and dry both the inside and outside. Cut four pieces of foil, leaving 4 inches of excess foil on each end of the fish. With your fingers, spread some butter on the foil. Place the fish in the center of the foil. Fill the cavities with some of the butter, reserving the remaining butter to smear on the outside of the fish. Bring the long sides of the foil up to meet, and then fold these over by ½-inch sections, leaving some space above the piece of fish for it to steam. Then fold up the ends as well, so the melted butter won't run out all over the place.

2. Place these individual cooking vessels containing the fish on a grill over low heat, and cook slowly for about 15 to 20 minutes. Check the fish after 10 minutes and then continuously after, to gauge the firmness. Larger fish will take up to 25 minutes. The skin should roll away easily from the flesh, and the flesh should flake easily away from the bones.

FOR THE LEMON-SAGE BUTTER

½ pound unsalted butter at room temperature

¼ cup chopped shallots

1 tablespoon finely grated lemon zest

1 tablespoon fresh lemon juice

2 tablespoons minced fresh sage leaves

½ teaspoon Kosher salt

1. In a mixing bowl, soften the butter, and using a wooden spoon, work the butter until pliable (like clay). Add the shallots, the lemon zest, lemon juice, minced fresh sage leaves, and salt, and mix until well incorporated. Transfer the butter to a sheet of wax paper, placing it in the center of the edge closest to you.

2. Fold the paper over the butter, and roll it into a uniform cylinder, about 1½ inches in diameter, and twist the ends to seal. Chill the butter in the refrigerator, or freeze for further use.

To Serve: Open the top of the foil package and, using a spoon, baste the fish with the melted butter a few times. Transfer the entire package to a plate and serve with a mixed green salad on the side and some boiled new potatoes and crunchy French bread to soak up the Lemon-Sage Butter.

"Casting upstream for trout is one of the most pleasant ways to spend an early summer morning, and cooking your catch is equally satisfying. With this recipe, you will be creating individual cooking vessels in which to steam the fish. The compound butter, which you can prepare in advance and bring to the campsite, elevates the fish from simple to simply great."

—CHEF CHARLIE PALMER

Roasted Hog Snapper

CHEF GRAHAM DAILEY | SERVES 4

"Different types of snapper taste different, depending on what they are eating and the environment they are living in. In my cooking, I cook a lot with cast iron pans, or outside grills, and just salt, pepper, and a little bit of lemon juice. I want to be able to taste those rich, natural flavors of the fish." —**CHEF GRAHAM DAILEY**

INGREDIENTS

Four 6-ounce hog snapper fillets
1 tablespoon Kosher salt, for
  blanching
16 to 20 asparagus spears
6 tablespoons canola oil, divided
Kosher salt and black pepper
1½ cups sliced leek, white and
  pale green parts only
1½ cups fresh sweet corn kernels,
  about 2 ears
6 ounces jumbo lump crabmeat
1 tablespoon diced red bell
  pepper
1½ tablespoons unsalted butter
2 tablespoons minced chives
½ cup Roasted Tomato
  Vinaigrette (recipe following)

1. Preheat the grill to high and
the oven to 375 degrees.

2. Bring a large pot of water
and 1 tablespoon Kosher salt to
a boil. Add the asparagus, and
cook just until tender, about 4
to 6 minutes. Transfer to a bowl
filled with ice water to stop the
cooking process, then drain.

3. In a bowl, toss the asparagus with 1 tablespoon of the
oil, season lightly with salt and
pepper, and place it on the grill.
Cook until lightly charred, turning

once, about 2 to 4 minutes per
side. Set aside.

4. Meanwhile, heat 2 tablespoons
of the oil in a large skillet over
medium-high heat. When the oil
is hot, add the leek and corn, and
sauté for 2 minutes. Add the crabmeat, and cook for 1 minute. Add
the red bell pepper, and cook to
warm them through, 1 to 2 minutes. Stir in the butter and chives,
and season with salt and pepper
taste. Remove from the heat, and
set aside.

5. In an oven-safe, nonstick
skillet, heat the remaining 3
tablespoons of oil over medium-
high heat. Season the snapper
fillet slightly on both sides with
salt and pepper. Add the fillets
to the pan, flesh side down, and
cook until golden brown, about
2 minutes. Turn the fillets over,
place the skillet in the oven, and
cook until the fish is just cooked
through, 4 to 6 minutes.

FOR THE ROASTED
TOMATO VINAIGRETTE
(yields 2 cups)
1 large tomato, quartered
1 teaspoon olive oil
Kosher salt and white pepper

1 clove garlic, crushed
1 teaspoon chopped fresh thyme
1 cup chopped shallot
1 cup chicken broth
½ cup white wine
2 teaspoons Champagne vinegar
1 cup canola oil

Preheat the oven to 400 degrees.
Place the tomato on a sheet
pan, drizzle with the olive oil,
and season lightly with salt
and pepper. Roast until lightly
charred, about 20 to 25 minutes.
In a medium saucepan, combine
everything except the vinegar and
canola oil, over medium heat.
Bring to a simmer, and cook until
the liquid reduces by half, about
10 to 15 minutes. Remove the
saucepan from the heat, stir in
the vinegar and oil, and using a
blender, purée the mixture until
smooth. Season with salt and
pepper, to taste.

To Serve: Divide the asparagus
and crab sauté among four plates.
Top each with a snapper fillet.
Drizzle with the Roasted Tomato
Vinaigrette.

Smoked Bacon Oyster Stew

CHEF GRAHAM DAILEY | SERVES 4

INGREDIENTS

20 oysters, shucked
1 cup diced smoked bacon
6 tablespoons diced green bell pepper
6 tablespoons diced red bell pepper
6 tablespoons diced yellow bell pepper
2 teaspoons diced shallots
2 teaspoons minced garlic
½ cup oyster liquor
1½ cups veal stock
⅔ cup heavy cream
2 teaspoons diced basil
2 teaspoons minced chives
Salt and pepper, to taste

1. In a large shallow saucepan, cook the bacon over medium-high heat until crisp, then drain. Add the bell peppers, shallots, and garlic, and cook for 2 minutes. Add the oyster liquor, and cook until almost dry, about 2 to 4 minutes.

2. Add the veal stock to the pan, and cook until it achieves a sauce consistency, about 3 to 5 minutes. Add the cream, and cook until reduced by half, about 4 to 6 minutes.

3. Add the oysters, basil, and chives, and decrease the heat to low. Cook until the oysters are warmed through and their edges curl, about 2 to 4 minutes.

To Serve: Serve over simple buttery mashed potatoes or creamy grits.

TOASTING THE HUNT

Desserts & Drinks

Fire-Roasted Pineapple with Rum

CHEF CHARLIE PALMER | SERVES 4

INGREDIENTS

1 large pineapple, rind cut away
½ cup cold water
½ cup granulated sugar
½ cup firmly packed light
   brown sugar
1 teaspoon pure vanilla extract
½ cup dark rum

1. Split the pineapple, lengthwise, into quarters. Carefully slice off any of the hard core. Place the pieces of pineapple in a high-sided plastic container that has a lid, and set aside.

2. In a saucepan, combine the water, granulated sugar, brown sugar, and vanilla extract, and bring to a simmer. Cook, stirring, until all of the sugar has dissolved, which should take no more than a minute. Remove from the heat, and stir in the rum.

3. Pour the rum syrup over the pineapple, turning each piece to coat all sides. Cover, and refrigerate for 12 hours or up to 2 days. Shake the container periodically to rotate the pineapple so each piece gets a good coating of the syrup.

4. When ready to grill, remove the pineapple from the container, reserving the syrup, and place on the grill just to the side of the main heat of the fire. If grilled over high heat, the added sugar in the rum syrup absorbed by the pineapple will cause it to burn before cooking through.

5. Grill for 10 to 15 minutes, turning every 3 to 4 minutes, until all sides are lightly charred and caramelized.

6. While the pineapple is grilling, transfer the reserved marinade to a small saucepan. When placing over an open fire, pay extra attention because the raw alcohol can ignite. Bring the syrup to a boil, then lower the heat, and simmer for 10 to 15 minutes. Remove from the heat, and set aside.

To Serve: Remove the pineapple from the grill and cut into thick slices. Serve over Spiced Molasses Pound Cake (page 244) or ice cream with the rum syrup drizzled liberally over.

"Hunters and anglers, or hikers and foragers, we all find that it's the time spent together that makes our campfire meals more rewarding."

—CHEF CHARLIE PALMER

Cast Iron Upside-Down
Apple Pie with Vanilla Ice Cream

CHEF BRIAN MERCURY | SERVES 6-8

INGREDIENTS

8 Braeburn apples, peeled, cored,
    and quartered
10½ ounces granulated sugar
4¼ ounces butter
1 puff pastry sheet (can purchase
    from supermarket)
Vanilla ice cream (recipe following)

For the Ice Cream

2 cups milk
2 cups heavy cream
1 pinch salt
8 ounces sugar
1 vanilla bean
7 ounces egg yolks

1. For the ice cream, heat cream, milk, sugar, salt, and vanilla beans, and then temper some of the hot cream with egg yolks. Bring cream mixture to a boil and add yolks, cook for 30 seconds. Strain through fine mesh strainer in to a metal pan in ice bath, and cool completely. Freeze in ice cream freezer and save for assembly.

2. Roll out one sheet of puff pastry sheet out to ¼ inch thick, and cut out a circle to match the diameter of a 9-inch cast iron pan. Wrap the dough and place in the refrigerator to chill.

3. Heat a medium-sized saucepan on high, and warm the sugar in it. Cook the sugar through until it begins to caramelize. Cook until it reaches a nice amber color.

4. Add the apples to the browned sugar and stir to them to completely coat. Leave them over the heat another 30 to 60 minutes until warmed through, then remove from the heat and set aside.

5. Grease a cast iron pan well, and place the apples slices in a circle around the bottom of the pan, their flat sides down; be sure to fit them all in, as a tighter fit helps the tart stay together after baking. Scrape all the caramel on top of apples, and allow it cool slightly.

6. Remove the dough from the refrigerator, remove the wrapping, and dock the dough with a fork. Lay the dough on top of the apples, tucking it around the outside edges of the apples to cover them well. Bake at 375 degrees for 45 minutes.

To Serve: Remove the finished pie from oven and let cool for 5 to 10 minutes. To serve, place a plate of a diameter 1 or 2 inches larger than the cast iron pan over the baked dough, and carefully invert this to release the pie from the pan. Be careful in doing this, as some of the still-hot juices may spill out and the crust will still be fragile. Serve slices of the finished pie with ice cream, and enjoy!

Grandma's Wyoming Whoppers

CHEF BRIAN MERCURY | YIELDS 12 COOKIES

INGREDIENTS

⅔ cup butter
1¼ cup dark brown sugar
¾ cup granulated sugar
3 eggs
1½ cup chunky peanut butter
Pinch of salt
6 cups rolled oats
2 teaspoons baking soda
1½ cup golden raisins
2 cups bittersweet chocolate chips

1. Melt butter on low heat.

2. Blend the butter, brown sugar, sugar, eggs, peanut butter, and salt in a mixing bowl, stirring until smooth.

3. Add the oats, baking soda, raisins, and chocolate chips. Mix until well combined.

4. Drop or scoop the dough onto a parchment-lined sheet pan. Dampen your hands, and slightly flatten the dough. Sprinkle a little salt on top of each.

5. Bake at 325 degrees for 10 to 15 minutes. Then cool on wire rack, and serve.

Fearing's Banana Pudding

CHEF DEAN FEARING | SERVES 6

INGREDIENTS

1¼ cups heavy cream
1 vanilla bean
15 egg yolks
¾ cup sugar
Salt, to taste
2 bananas, sliced

1. In a medium saucepan over medium heat, add ¼-inch water to the pan. Separately, heat the cream and vanilla bean in a medium saucepan over medium heat, to a steady simmer.

2. Place a large stainless-steel mixing bowl in the pan with the water, creating a double boiler. Add the yolks and sugar, whisking continuously to a ribbon consistency, about 3 minutes. Turn up the heat for the cream and bring it to a boil. Adding the cream in a small stream, mix and temper it into the yolks, whisking continuously to combine, forming the pudding.

3. Remove the bowl from the double boiler, and pour the prepared pudding through a fine sieve. Transfer the pudding to a container, and cool in the refrigerator or in an ice bath. Once cooled, cover the pudding. The pudding may be portioned out as needed and will hold in the refrigerator for three days.

To Serve: In a medium mixing bowl, combine the bananas and the pudding, folding these together gently. Scoop equal amounts of the pudding into six small glass bowls and serve.

‹ *Pecan Tart*

CHEF HAL ROWLAND | SERVES 4

INGREDIENTS

¼ cup sugar
½ cup butter
1 large egg yolk
⅛ teaspoon salt
1¼ cups all-purpose flour
Tart Filling (recipe following)

For the Tart Filling

3 whole eggs
½ cup (packed) brown sugar
½ cup maple syrup
½ cup dark corn syrup
½ cup unsalted butter
⅛ teaspoon salt
1½ cups chopped pecans

1. Start by making the dough. Cream the sugar and butter, add eggs, beat until fluffy, then add the dry ingredients slowly until mixed. Refrigerate for 30 minutes.

2. For the filling: Melt the butter, add the rest of the ingredients in a bowl, and mix together well. Reserve.

3. Remove dough from the refrigerator. Roll out the tart dough until flat. Place the dough evenly in four tartlet molds, and bake to 50 percent doneness. Add the filling, and cook at 350 degrees for 40 minutes.

🎙 *"They call me Bubba Crocker. I make banana nut bread, my wife's sour cream pound cake, and old Southern staples like ginger snaps, banana pudding, and ambrosia."* —CHEF HAL ROWLAND

Sticky Toffee Pudding

CHEF ROB MCDANIEL | SERVES 8

INGREDIENTS

1 cup plus 2 tablespoons
   all-purpose flour
2 teaspoons baking powder,
   divided
¾ cup pitted dates
1¼ cups boiling water
¼ cup unsalted butter, softened
¾ cup granulated sugar
1 large egg, lightly beaten
1 teaspoon vanilla
Toffee Sauce (recipe following)

For the Toffee Sauce

½ cup unsalted butter
½ cup heavy cream
1 cup packed light brown sugar
1 cup heavy cream, whipped
Mint, for garnish

1. Preheat oven to 350 degrees. Butter the eight aluminum cupcake liners. Sift the flour and one teaspoon of the baking powder into a bowl, and set aside. Chop the dates into a small bowl along with the remaining teaspoon of baking powder, and cover with the boiling water. Set aside.

2. In a standing mixer, cream the sugar and butter until nice and fluffy; add the eggs and vanilla, mixing these in until blended. Gradually mix in the flour-baking powder mixture. Once this has been incorporated, remove from mixer, and using a spatula, incorporate the date mixture.

3. Portion this evenly into the buttered cups, and bake for 15 to 20 minutes until the tops are firm. Remove these from the oven, and allow to cool.

4. Combine the butter, brown sugar, and heavy cream in a heavy-bottomed saucepan. Heat until it begins to boil, stirring constantly, then turn down to simmer over medium-low heat, until the mixture thickens.

To Serve: If the puddings are cool, place them in a warm oven to gently heat them through. Remove from the cupcake liners, and place them individually on small serving plates; spoon toffee sauce over each. Top each with whipped cream, and garnish with the mint if desired.

Spiced Molasses Pound Cake

CHEF CHARLIE PALMER | YIELDS ONE 9 BY 5-INCH LOAF

INGREDIENTS

2 cups sifted cake flour
2 teaspoons baking powder
1 teaspoon ground cinnamon
½ teaspoon ground nutmeg
¼ teaspoon ground cloves
¼ teaspoon freshly ground
 black pepper
8 tablespoons (1 stick) unsalted
 butter, at room temperature
½ cup sugar
2 extra-large eggs
½ cup blackstrap molasses
 (unsulfured)
⅔ cup whole milk
Caramel Sauce (recipe following)

1. Preheat the oven to 350 degrees. Grease a 9 by 5-inch loaf pan with butter, lightly flour, and set aside.

2. Sift together the dry ingredients, and set aside.

3. Using a wooden spoon or a stand mixer fitted with the paddle attachment, cream together the butter and sugar. Add the eggs and beat until well incorporated. Stir in the molasses.

4. Mix half the dry ingredients into the creamed mixture, then add half of the milk. Repeat, incorporating all of the ingredients.

5. Pour the batter into the prepared pan, and bake until a toothpick inserted into the center of the cake comes out clean and the sides of the cake have pulled away from the edges of the pan, 40 to 50 minutes.

6. Cool for 15 minutes in the pan, then turn out onto a wire rack, and let cool completely.

FOR THE CARAMEL SAUCE

(yields 4 cups)
1 cup packed light brown sugar
¾ cup granulated sugar
1 cup cold water
¼ cup corn syrup
1 tablespoon fresh lemon juice
1 tablespoon pure vanilla extract
1½ cups heavy cream
2 tablespoons unsalted butter

1. In a heavy saucepan, combine the sugars with the cold water, and bring to a boil over medium heat. Boil for 12 minutes, or until the syrup is a rich caramel color, brushing down the sides of the pan with a wet pastry brush from time to time to dissolve any sugar crystals that form.

2. Taking care, as the syrup may bubble over, whisk in the corn syrup, lemon juice, and vanilla, and allow the mixture to come back up to a simmer. Carefully whisk in the cream, bring to a boil, and boil gently for 10 minutes, or until the sauce is thick. Whisk in the butter, and serve hot. The sauce will keep, tightly covered and refrigerated, for about 2 weeks. Reheat before serving.

To Serve: Cut the cake into thick slices and top with Caramel sauce or Fire Roasted Pineapples with Rum (Page 238).

Banana Sandie

CHEF CHARLIE PALMER | SERVES 4

INGREDIENTS

2 cups crushed graham
cracker crumbs

4 bananas, peeled and split
lengthwise

One 1.55-ounce dark chocolate
bar, broken up

4 marshmallows, cut horizontally
into thirds

4 caramels (regular or sea salt),
quartered

Favorite ice cream, for serving

1. Mound ½ cup of crumbs in the center of each of four 12-inch squares of heavy-duty aluminum foil. Nestle two banana halves into each crumb mound, cut side down, and divide the chocolate, marshmallow, and caramel over the bananas. Gather the edges of the aluminum foil over the ingredients, and fold down to seal, keeping a pocket of air over the ingredients so the toppings don't stick to the foil as they heat.

2. Place the packets at the edge of a low-heat grill, and cover. Leave until the crumbs have been lightly toasted, the bananas are warmed through, and the toppings are melted, about 15 minutes.

To Serve: Carefully open the foil packets, and top each with a scoop of ice cream. Serve directly in the foil packets.

Warm Banana Pudding

CHEF KEVIN GILLESPIE | SERVES 12

INGREDIENTS

2 cups half-and-half
2 cups whole milk
1 vanilla bean, split
1½ teaspoons vanilla extract
8 large eggs
2½ cups sugar
1 cup all-purpose flour
1 teaspoon salt
6 tablespoons butter, cut
    into chunks
1 store-bought loaf of pound cake,
    about 12 ounces
½ cup strong brewed coffee
8 to 9 very ripe bananas, peeled
    and cut into ½-inch coins
½ teaspoon cream of tartar

1. Preheat the oven to 375 degrees.

2. In a large saucepan, combine the half-and-half, milk, vanilla bean, and ½ teaspoon of the vanilla extract, and heat this over medium-high heat until bubbles start forming around the edges, about 4 minutes. Pull the pan from the heat. Remove the vanilla bean, and use a paring knife to scrape the vanilla bean's pulp from the pod into the milk mixture. Discard the pod.

3. Separate the egg yolks from the whites using the three-bowl method: one small bowl to separate the eggs over, one large bowl for the yolks, and a third bowl to collect all of the whites. Crack one egg at a time, straining the white into the small separating bowl and placing the yolk in the yolk bowl. If the yolk did not break, transfer the white to the white collection bowl. (This method ensures that no broken yolk gets into the main batch of whites. If you break a yolk, you'll only lose one white instead of the whole batch. For meringue, it's imperative to have whites with absolutely no yolk in them, or the whites won't whip up properly.)

4. Add 2 cups of the sugar to the yolks and whisk until very thick and light yellow, about 1 minute. Pour the flour into a strainer over the yolk bowl and shake the flour into the yolks. Whisk the flour and salt into the egg yolks until smooth.

5. Slowly whisk ¾ cup of the milk mixture into the yolk mixture, to gradually warm the eggs so they won't scramble; this is called tempering. Whisk all the yolk mixture into the milk mixture and return the pan to medium heat. Cook the mixture until it thickens, about 8 minutes, stirring nonstop. There will be some lumps, which is fine.

6. Remove the pan from the heat and whisk in the butter, one piece at a time, until it's all incorporated. Blend the pudding with an immersion blender for 1 minute. Press the pudding through a fine-mesh strainer to remove any remaining lumps.

7. Slice the pound cake ¼-inch thick and arrange the slices in a single layer on a baking sheet. Toast these in the oven until they are lightly browned, about 6 minutes. Flip the slices, and toast again until lightly browned, about 4 minutes more. Remove the toasted cake from the oven, and brush both sides with the coffee.

8. Spoon about 1½ cups of the pudding into the bottom of a 2-quart, deep casserole dish. Layer the pound cake and bananas on top of the pudding, then repeat the process, ending with a layer of pudding.

9. In a small bowl, whisk the remaining ½ cup sugar and cream of tartar to combine. Whip the egg whites in a mixer fitted with a whisk attachment until they are thick and frothy, about 2 minutes. With the mixer running, slowly add the sugar mixture to the egg whites. Add the remaining 1 teaspoon vanilla extract, and beat until the mixture holds soft peaks when the whisk is lifted.

To Serve: Mound the meringue on top of the pudding, and spread to completely cover and seal at the edges. Using the back of a spoon, swirl the meringue into peaks. Bake at 375 until the peaks are browned, about 5 minutes. The top should be browned while the center of the meringue stays soft and creamy. Let the dish cool for at least 15 minutes. Serve warm.

Ice Cream Sandwiches

PASTRY CHEF PAMELA MOXLEY | YIELDS 14 DOZEN COOKIES

Chef's Note: Recipe may be cut in half, if necessary. The same preparation process is used for both the blondie cookie and the chocolate cookie.

BLONDIE COOKIE

5½ cups all-purpose flour
1 teaspoon baking soda
2 teaspoons salt
1 pound unsalted butter, divided
1½ cups dark brown sugar
1½ cups granulated sugar
4 eggs
1 teaspoon vanilla extract

CHOCOLATE COOKIE

4 cups cake flour
2 cups all-purpose flour
1 pound unsalted butter, divided
2 cups granulated sugar
4 eggs
1 tablespoon vanilla
1½ cups cocoa powder
2 teaspoons baking soda
1 teaspoon salt

1. Preheat the oven to 250 degrees. In a large bowl, sift together the dry ingredients.

2. In a small saucepan, over medium heat, melt half the butter. Add the brown sugar, and cook until the sugar melts and the ingredients are well combined. Set aside.

3. In a large bowl, using a paddle attachment for a mixer, cream together the remaining butter with the granulated sugar. Add eggs, one at a time, mixing well.

4. In another large bowl, using a spatula, add the warm butter mixture to dry ingredients, and mix well. Combine this with the creamed mixture, and mix well to create the dough.

5. Chill the dough for at least 2 hours. Roll out onto Silpats or silicone baking sheets, using plastic wrap to get the dough as thin and even as possible, about ¼ inch.

6. Bake for 4 to 5 minutes. Once cool, but still slightly warm, cut into 3-inch-by-7-inch rectangles.

To Serve: Fill with desired ice cream to create your sandwiches.

Fall Fruit Cast Iron Crisp

CHEF DAVID GUAS | SERVES 6-8

Chef's Note: This recipe is built for "Lili," the 12-inch Butter Pat Industries cast iron pan.

INGREDIENTS

8 ounces light brown sugar
1½ tablespoons all-purpose flour
1½ teaspoons Kosher salt
4 ounces pecan pieces, lightly toasted, cooled
1½ ounces butter, cold and cubed
1½ pounds Honeycrisp apples, peeled, cored, sliced ⅛-inch thick
1½ pounds Bartlett pears, firm, peeled, cored, sliced ⅛-inch thick
2 tablespoons fresh lemon juice
¼ cup light brown sugar
1 teaspoon cinnamon, ground
1 teaspoon nutmeg, freshly grated
3 tablespoons honey, wildflower or tupelo
2 tablespoons bourbon
1½ tablespoons tapioca flour or cornstarch

1. Preheat oven to 350 degrees. Using room temperature butter, brush the inside of a 12-inch cast iron pan, and reserve.

2. In a food processor, combine the sugar, flour, salt, and cooled pecans, and pulse a few times. Add the cold, cubed butter, and pulse again until the mixture is coarse but not too lumpy. Transfer the topping mixture to a bowl, and reserve in the refrigerator until ready to bake.

3. In a large mixing bowl, combine the apples and pears and the other remaining ingredients, and gently toss together until everything is evenly mixed.

4. Transfer the apple-pear mixture to the buttered cast iron pan. Sprinkle the chilled and reserved topping mixture over the fruit mixture.

5. Bake in the center of your oven for approximately an hour. The fruit should be bubbling, and the crumble should be nicely browned.

6. Remove the crisp from the oven, and allow to cool for 20 to 30 minutes before serving.

"I always joke about food tasting better when I use my cast iron, but it really does. Cast iron pans have been here long before us, and they will be here after us—and for good reason. The beauty of cast iron is that it's not going anywhere. So even if this trend dies down or we move on to something else, it will still be there. And it will be that much more important to me in my daily life and in my restaurants to keep the traditions alive for my kids and grandkids. So that one day they will be cooking my recipes in my old cast iron pan."

—CHEF DAVID GUAS

Tiramisu

LINDA FISHER | SERVES 9

INGREDIENTS

6 large egg yolks
1 cup sugar
1¼ cup mascarpone cheese,
    room temperature
1¾ cup heavy whipping cream
Two 7-ounce packages Italian
    ladyfingers
1 cup cold espresso
½ cup coffee-flavored liqueur,
    optional
1 ounce cocoa for dusting

1. In a double boiler over boiling water, combine egg yolks and sugar. Reduce the heat to low, and continue cooking for about 10 minutes, stirring constantly. Remove the pan from the heat, and whip the mixture until the yolks are thick and lemon-colored.

2. Add the mascarpone to the whipped yolks, beating until combined. (The mascarpone does not have to be exactly at room temperature. Take it out of the refrigerator as you begin gathering ingredients.)

3. In a separate bowl, whip the heavy cream to stiff peaks. Gently fold the whipped cream into the mascarpone sabayon mixture and set aside.

4. Mix the cold espresso with the coffee liqueur, and dip the ladyfingers into the mixture just long enough to get them wet. (Do not soak them!) Arrange the prepared ladyfingers in the bottom of a 9-inch square baking dish (or another container, similarly sized).

5. Spoon half the mascarpone cream filling into the baking dish over the ladyfingers, repeating this process with another layer of ladyfingers and cream.

6. Refrigerate 4 hours or overnight, before serving.

Chef's Note: The tiramisu recipe can also be prepared in individual serving dishes (right) instead of a large dish, with additional garnishes.

‹ *Hemingway Daiquiri with Luxardo*
FRED MINNICK

INGREDIENTS
2 ounces light rum
¾ ounce fresh lime juice
½ ounce fresh grapefruit juice
½ ounce Luxardo

Note: Most recipes call for a Maraschino liqueur, but there's only one worth putting in your cocktail shaker and that's Luxardo.

Combine all ingredients with ice in a shaker and shake until you see flecks of ice on the outside of the tin. Strain into a cocktail glass and garnish with a lime wheel.

Champion's Sunset
FROM THE BARTENDERS AT CHAMPIONS RETREAT IN EVANS, GA

INGREDIENTS
1 ounce El Jimador tequila
   reposado
1 ounce Bombay Sapphire gin
¾ ounce Combier orange liqueur
¾ ounce Aperol
½ ounce ruby red grapefruit syrup
¼ ounce fresh-squeezed Meyer
   lemon juice
¼ ounce fresh-squeezed Key
   lime juice

Combine all ingredients into a cocktail shaker, completely filled with ice. Shake vigorously for 15 seconds. Take a lemon twist, and rub it along the rim of a chilled martini glass. Strain shaker contents into the martini glass.

To Serve: Garnish with a lime wedge.

Brown Derby
FRED MINNICK

INGREDIENTS
2 ounces bourbon
1 ounce of freshly squeezed
   grapefruit juice
Honey syrup

Combine all ingredients into a cocktail shaker. Shake well, and strain. Serve in chilled glass without ice.

The Arnold

FROM THE BARTENDERS AT CHAMPIONS RETREAT IN EVANS, GA

INGREDIENTS

Almost 2 ounces Fruitland
Augusta Peach Tea Vodka
1 ounce Russo Limoncello
1 ounce hibiscus tea extract
1 ounce Fever-Tree Bitter Lemon
   soda
1 ounce pure organic cane syrup

Combine all ingredients except the lemon soda in a cocktail shaker completely filled with ice. Shake vigorously for 15 seconds. Strain over fresh ice into a Collins glass, stopping 1 inch from the top of the glass. Top off with Fever-Tree Bitter Lemon soda.

To Serve: Garnish with lemon and lime wedges.

Salty Saint Bernard

CHEF GRAHAM DAILEY

INGREDIENTS

2 lime wedges
1½ ounces freshly squeezed ruby
   red grapefruit juice
1½ ounces pink grapefruit vodka
1½ ounces elderflower liqueur

Rub the rim of a chilled pilsner glass with one of the limes, then dip the rim in salt. Combine the vodka and grapefruit juice in a cocktail shaker filled with ice. Shake until chilled, and strain into the pilsner glass. Top with the elderflower liqueur. Garnish with the remaining lime wedge.

The Gold Rush ❯

FRED MINNICK

INGREDIENTS

1½ ounces Domaine de Canton
1 ounce bourbon
½ ounce fresh lemon juice

Combine all ingredients into a cocktail shaker. Shake and pour over ice.

🖺 *"In the right hands, bar tools, fruit, and whiskey can yield one of life's great pleasures as you sip. But cocktails are only as good as the bartender's skill. That's why one Manhattan's sublime texture and rich bourbon balance stands out over another's cherry juice-saturated mediocrity. As drinkers, we remember our favorite bartenders and follow them from place to place. We can also dabble at home. It's time to take your love of the cocktail into your own hands, and start mixing."* **—FRED MINNICK**

"As an artist and craftsman, I wanted to honor a life beyond just the limiting of my harvests, and use items I collected in fields and forests to complement my dishes and drinks. So years ago I began using the pieces I gathered in the woods, such as bones and feathers, to make distinct and purposeful works of art. For example, I tie various bird feathers to toothpicks to place in cocktails, and use pheasant and larger bird feathers to make ink pens. I give them as gifts to those who were kind enough to invite me to beautiful places where I had the opportunity to experience life and create special memories. This is a particularly fun and thoughtful way to honor harvests. I challenge you to channel your inner artist. I find that it is not complicated, a lot of fun, and truly impactful.

In giving someone a gift—made with your own hands, from the place you hunted together and the birds harvested—you realize that while the bird may have died months or even years before, it has found new life, and lives today for those who see it and touch it and those you share it with. It is an homage to the hope of a life well lived, in the outdoors, and those who live in it."

—CHRIS HASTINGS
Chef and Outdoorsman

The Player

FROM THE BARTENDERS AT CHAMPIONS RETREAT IN EVANS, GA

INGREDIENTS

2½ ounces Virgil Kaine rye
½ ounce La Quintinye "Royal Rouge" sweet vermouth
¼ ounce La Quintinye dry vermouth
¼ ounce Luxardo cherry liqueur
Splash fresh-squeezed orange juice
3 dashes Suze Orange Bitters

In a whiskey glass, add one large ice cube, preferably 2-by-2 inches. Slowly pour rye over the ice cube, followed (in this order) sweet vermouth, dry vermouth, Luxardo, orange juice, and Suze Orange Bitters. Gently stir 15 complete turns with a bar spoon.

To Serve: Garnish with a Makers Mark or Luxardo cherry.

Manhattan

FRED MINNICK

INGREDIENTS

2 ounces rye
1 ounce Italian vermouth
2 dashes Angostura bitters (no substituting, it must be Angostura)

Note: To make this a "perfect Manhattan," use ½ ounce Italian vermouth and ½ ounce French vermouth.

Stir rye, vermouth, and bitters in cracked ice until your tin ices over.

❮ Bog Sucker

CHEF CHRIS HASTINGS

INGREDIENTS

¼ cup vodka, well chilled
2 tablespoons dry sherry, well chilled
1 green olive, skewered with a hawthorn

Combine the vodka and sherry in a martini shaker filled halfway with ice. Shake until the mixture is well chilled. Strain into an old-fashioned glass filled with ice and garnish with the olive-skewered hawthorn. Serve immediately.

🍸 *"Bog Sucker is another name for the woodcock. This is the classic post-woodcock hunt beverage. I was introduced to this libation by Frank Harris in Louisiana."* —**CHEF CHRIS HASTINGS**

Odd Job "1696"

INGREDIENTS

Vodka infused with saffron, Galliano L'Autentico, amber vermouth, orange oil

Le Chiffre

INGREDIENTS

Beluga vodka, Rosehip Cup liqueur, orange liqueur, vodka infused with chili, orange zest

The Classic Vesper

INGREDIENTS

Gin, vodka, Angostura bitters, amber vermouth, orange zest

RECIPES FROM THE BARTENDERS AT DUKES HOTEL AND BAR IN LONDON, UK

"At Dukes Hotel, we only stir, to keep the clarity and flavor. Saying that, in the 1950s cocktails were only ever served as an apéritif before dinner, and it was seen to be a real faux pas to mix two white spirits. Not so with Bond, though. For a drink to be a cocktail, it needs three ingredients. Gin, tonic, and lemon, for example. The same is true for a good bartender. They must have three ingredients: to be diplomatic, acrobatic, and charismatic."

—ALESSANDRO PALAZZI, HEAD BARTENDER AT DUKES BAR

❮ *Sidecar with Grand Marnier*
FRED MINNICK

INGREDIENTS

1 ounce Cognac
¾ ounce Grand Marnier
¾ ounce lemon juice

Add all ingredients in a cocktail shaker with ice and vigorously shake. Strain over ice.

Old Fashioned
FRED MINNICK

INGREDIENTS

1 sugar cube
3 dashes Angostura bitters
Club soda
2 ounces rye or bourbon whiskey

Place sugar in an Old Fashioned glass, then add three dashes of bitters and a splash of club soda. Muddle the sugar, rotate the glass to line it with the sugar mixture, and add a large ice cube. Pour the whiskey. Garnish the drink with an orange twist, if you'd like.

Rufus Horneros
FROM THE BARTENDERS AT OVENBIRD IN BIRMINGHAM, AL

INGREDIENTS

2 ounces Old Overholt
  Rye Whiskey
1 teaspoon Pecan Syrup (recipe
  following)
2 dashes Scrappy's Chocolate
  Bitters
2 dashes Angostura bitters

Add ingredients in mixing glass, then stir. Strain into "rufus" glass over ice. Express orange over cocktail, then garnish with orange peel and cherry.

For the Pecan Syrup: The pecan syrup is made by first roasting pecans in an oven until toasted. Then combine with a 2:1 ratio of demerara sugar (a coarse, raw sugar from Guyana, with pronounced caramel flavors) and water.

Toasted Old Fashioned ❯

MERCEDES O'BRIEN, BARTENDER AT GUNSHOW IN ATLANTA, GA

INGREDIENTS

2 dashes aromatic bitters
(Angostura or Fee's Old
Fashioned)
2 dashes orange bitters
¼ ounce burnt sugar syrup
(recipe following)
2 ounces bourbon
Sugared Cinnamon Sticks (recipe
following)

1. Add the bitters, syrup, and
bourbon to a rocks glass. Add ice
until a slight sheen appears on the
outside of the glass.

2. Garnish with Sugared Cinnamon Sticks on the side, drizzle
with 151 rum, and light it on fire.

3. Express an orange peel over the
flame, and let this cook until the
sugars in it bubble.

4. Blow out the flame, then nudge
each cinnamon stick into a glass
using the orange peel. To finish,
wipe the orange oils on the rim of
the glass, and place the peel perpen-
dicular across the cinnamon stick.

*FOR THE BURNT
SUGAR SYRUP*

8 cups sugar
4 cups water

Cook the sugar in a pan over
medium-high heat, not stirring at
first, until it begins to turn gold-
brown around the edges. Then
stir to incorporate the melted
(liquid) sugar. Continue heating
and stirring until all the sugar is
melted through and it achieves
an amber color and a liquid
consistency. Remove from heat,
and allow to cool for about 10

minutes. Slowly add the water
until well incorporated, being
very careful to avoid splattering.
Let cool.

Chef's Note: The syrup can be kept
over time in the fridge for up to
one month.

*FOR THE SUGARED
CINNAMON STICKS*

Cinnamon sticks
Bourbon, to coat
Sugar, to coat

Add the cinnamon sticks to a
small bowl and coat them lightly
with some bourbon. Layer a
cookie sheet with sugar, and place
the damp cinnamon sticks on top.
Cover these with an additional
layer of sugar, and then let them
sit overnight in a cool, dry place.

Whiskey Sour

FRED MINNICK

INGREDIENTS

1 ounce fresh-squeezed lemon juice
1 tablespoon caster sugar
1 egg white
1½ ounces grain-forward bourbon

Add all of the ingredients to a shaker filled with ice and shake. Strain into
a rocks glass filled with fresh ice. Garnish with a cherry and lemon wedge.

CONTRIBUTORS

Recipes from the following chefs and culinary professionals: Kipp Bourdeau, Mercedes O'Brien, Denny Corriveau, Tim Creehan, Graham Dailey, Josh Drage, Dean Fearing, Sean Finley, Linda Fisher, Ben Ford, Gianni Gallucci, Kevin Gillespie, David Guas, Gordon Hamersley, Chris Hastings, Angelia Highsmith, Anthony Lamas, Ruthie Landelius, Scott Leysath, Joseph Lenn, Doug Mack, Rob McDaniel, Brian Mercury, Fred Minnick, Pamela Moxley, Scott Ostrander, Charlie Palmer, Hal Rowland, Steven Satterfield, Leslie Shepherd, Frank Stitt

Photographs: Terry Allen, Kenneth Boone, Kevin Garrett, Brian Grossenbacher, John Hafner, Kay Heritage, Tyler Sharp, Mike Schalk, Carl Tremblay
Illustrations: Virginia England, Katherine Gobel, Russ Grimes
Cover photograph: Tyler Sharp

Feature stories: Miles DeMott, Addy McDaniel, Tyler Sharp
Additional contributions: Jocelyn Thames

Special thanks: Chris Hastings, Kevin Gillespie, Graham Dailey, Reid Bryant, Brian Grossenbacher

CHEF INDEX

Chefs and their recipes featured throughout Volumes 1 through 6 in Covey Rise magazine.

TIM CREEHAN

Inlet Beach, Florida | Cuvee 30A
Featured in February-March 2013 (Covey Rise Volume 1, Number 2) "Great Game"
Recipes: Venison Short-Loin Filet with Tomato Basil Butter Sauce 97; Lamb Osso Buco 102; Crisp Boneless Duck 135; Pheasant on Red Cabbage and Cranberries with Roasted Vegetables and Wilted Spinach 150

GORDON HAMERSLEY

Boston, Massachusetts | Food Columnist for The Boston Globe
Featured in June-July 2013 (Covey Rise Volume 1, Number 4) "Boston Bistro"
Recipes: Grilled Quail Salad with Strawberries, Aged Balsamic Vinegar and Marcona Almonds 36; Ragout of Quail with Summer Vegetables and Basil Pesto 136; Roasted Quail with Peas, Morels, and Parmesan Risotto 157; Roasted Quail with Prosciutto, Red Onions, and Burnt Peaches 163

KIPP BOURDEAU

Okeechobee, Florida | Personal Chef/Assistant for Gene Reed Enterprise
Featured in August-September 2013 (Covey Rise Volume 1, Number 5) "Born to Cook"
Recipes: Tomahawk Ribeye Steak with Tomato Salad and Duck Fat Fries 96; Venison Medallions with Mushroom Risotto and Sweet Pepper Coulis 107; Seared Scallops with Wine Cheddar Grits, Sweet Corn Chowder, and Pulled Barbecue Pork Tenderloin 230

ROB MCDANIEL

Alexander City, Alabama | Springhouse
Featured in December-January 2013 (Covey Rise Volume 2, Number 1) "Springhouse"
Recipes: Smoked Scamp West Indies Salad 44; Beet and Radish Salad with Orange Vinaigrette 51; Rabbit Soup 106; Smoked Quail Terrine 171; Sticky Toffee Pudding 243

DENNY CORRIVEAU
Amesbury, Massachusetts | Wildcheff.com
Featured in December-January 2016 (Covey Rise Volume 4, Number 1) "At Home with the Wild Cheff"
Recipes: Cinnamon & Chili Rubbed Woodcock Salad 23; Apple & Sage Chukar Sausage 28; Sagebrush & Parmesan Grouse Meatballs 50; Bacon-Wrapped Maple Quail with Corn Succotash 126; Pheasant Applejack 139; Ginger Citrus Baked Woodcock 161; Southwestern Blue Corn Pheasant with Fruit Salsa 180; Grouse Penne in a Morel & Parmesan Cream Sauce 185

SEAN FINLEY
Pierre, South Dakota | Cheyenne Ridge
Featured in February-March 2016 (Covey Rise Volume 4, Number 2) "Consistency and Dedication"
Recipes: Beer-Braised Buffalo Short Ribs 76; Slow Smoked Beef Brisket 92; Buffalo Pheasant Wonton Cups 134; Pheasant Burger 146; Smoked Pheasant Flatbread Pizza 176; Crab-Stuffed Portobella Caps 215

SCOTT LEYSATH
Northern California | Sportingchef.com
Featured in April-May 2016 (Covey Rise Volume 4, Number 3) "Sporting Skill"
Recipes: Duck Stir Fry 141; Pheasant Leg Stew 148; Pheasant Street Taco 152; Roasted Quail with Pheasant Sausage Stuffing 158

GRAHAM DAILEY
Key West, Florida | Cafe Marquesa
Featured in June-July 2016 (Covey Rise Volume 4, Number 4) "A Chef's Artistic Vigil"
Recipes: Argentinian-Style Pheasant Tartare with Rye Toast, Capers, Tomato, and Basil Oil 30; Pan-Seared Soft Shell Crab BLT with Arugula and Roasted Tomato Butter 216; Pan-Seared Nantucket Bay Scallops with Roasted Cauliflower and Prosciutto 218; Roasted Hog Snapper 234; Smoked Bacon Oyster Stew 235; Salty Saint Bernard 260

DEAN FEARING
Dallas, Texas | Fearing's Restaurant
Featured in August-September 2016 (Covey Rise Volume 4, Number 5) "Born into the Business"
Recipes: Maple and Black-Peppercorn Soaked Buffalo Tenderloin 87; Barbecue Bacon-Wrapped Quail 128; Chicken Fried Lockhart Texas Quail on Jalapeño Creamed Corn 187; Barbecue Shrimp Taco with Mango Pickled Red Onion Salad 219; Fearing's Banana Pudding 241

HAL ROWLAND
Evans, Georgia | Champions Retreat
Featured in December-January 2017 (Covey Rise Volume 5, Number 1) "Food of Champions"
Recipes: Pork Shanks 94; Pecan Tart 243

GIANNI GALLUCCI
Chicago, Illinois | Zero Ottantuno
Featured in August-September 2017 (Covey Rise Volume 5, Number 5) "Pizza Oven Afield"
Recipes: Mozzarella Wrapped with Speck 28; Paccheri Bolognese 85; Quail Egg Pizza 154; Wood-Fired Quail 179

BEN FORD
Los Angeles, California | Ford's Filling Station
Featured in October-November 2017 (Covey Rise Volume 5, Number 6) "Cast Iron Cooking"
Recipes: Bacon-Wrapped Quail with Pickled Jalapeño Stuffing 125

DAVID GUAS
Arlington, Virginia | Bayou Bakery, Coffee Bar & Eatery
Featured in October-November 2017 (Covey Rise Volume 5, Number 6) "Cast Iron Cooking"
Recipes: Eastern Shore Goose Jerky 31; Buttermilk Biscuits with Goose Breakfast Sausage 165; Fall Fruit Cast Iron Crisp 252

BRIAN MERCURY
Boston, Massachusetts | Oak + Rowan
Featured in October-November 2017 (Covey Rise Volume 5, Number 6) "Cast Iron Cooking"
Recipes: Aunt Esta's Dinner Rolls 46; Cast Iron Upside-Down Apple Pie with Vanilla Ice Cream 240; Grandma's Wyoming Whoppers 241

KEVIN GILLESPIE
Atlanta, Georgia | Gunshow
Featured in February-March 2018 (Covey Rise Volume 6, Number 2) "Welcome to the Gunshow"
Recipes: Elk Vindaloo 78; Ground Venison Kabobs with Tomato Jam 99; Grilled Whitetail Filet 102; Wild Bird Fricassee 173; Warm Banana Pudding 248

JOSH DRAGE
Philipsburg, Montana | The Ranch at Rock Creek
Featured in April-May 2018 (Covey Rise Volume 6, Number 3) "Ranch at Rock Creek"
Recipes: Braised Elk Chuck Roast with Puttanesca Sauce 82; Buttermilk Tabasco Chicken 186; Aquavit Smoked Trout 214; Fresh Trout with Horseradish and Lemon Zest 226; Smoked Fish Potato Cake 231

FRED MINNICK
Louisville, Kentucky | Fredminnick.com
Featured "Toasting the Hunt" columnist in Covey Rise *magazine*
Recipes: Brown Derby 259; Hemingway Daiquiri with Luxardo 259; The Gold Rush 260; Manhattan 265; Old Fashioned 269; Sidecar with Grand Marnier 269; Whiskey Sour 270

ANGELIA HIGHSMITH
Thomasville, Georgia | Pinckney Hill Plantation
Featured in June-July 2018 (Covey Rise Volume 6, Number 4) "Red Hills Savor"
Recipes: Grilled Duck Roulade with Sundried Tomatoes 39; Blackberry-Balsamic Glazed Quail 161

LESLIE SHEPHERD
Thomasville, Georgia | Loveridge Plantation
Featured in June-July 2018 (Covey Rise Volume 6, Number 4) "Red Hills Savor"
Recipes: Bradley's Circles 33; Sous-Vide Quail 124

RUTHIE LANDELIUS
Thomasville, Georgia | Longpine Plantation
Featured in June-July 2018 (Covey Rise Volume 6, Number 4) "Red Hills Savor"
Recipes: Scallion Cornbread Cake with Honey Soy Drizzle and Fried Quail Egg 24; Quail Potstickers with Ponzu Sauce 26

INDEX

WESTERN ISLES WOODCOCK

A hunter heads to Scotland's Outer Hebrides
to test his sporting prowess against the wily
and wondrous woodcock.

STORY BY SIMON F. BARR
PHOTOGRAPHY BY TWEED MEDIA

COVEY RISE 286

About *Covey Rise* Magazine

Covey Rise *delivers the best of the upland sporting lifestyle to an international audience. Carefully crafted with extraordinary words and images, each issue* of Covey Rise *offers a glimpse of the constituent parts of the upland hunting experience, from dogs on point and scaling various terrains in search of wild birds to exploring fine guns and the artisans behind bespoke sporting products. Readers taste the game dishes of award-winning chefs in search of culinary treasures, toast the hunt with great wines, and treat themselves to bourbon and cigars, as the conversation drifts from the field to the table and beyond.*

With each issue, readers revel in the notion that the upland spirit is more than just flush and bang. It's about time spent afield with happy dogs in joyful pursuit. It's about memories made and savored among friends old and new, while walking the fields in conversation, or seated around tables filled with a day's harvest of fresh perspective.

That's the way Covey Rise *defines the upland sporting lifestyle, and its mission is to deliver readers into the heart of that experience with each and every issue.*

coveyrisemagazine.com

GAME: THE CHEF'S FIELD TO TABLE COOKBOOK

From the Editors of Covey Rise

Published in 2018 by Welcome Books
A Division of Rizzoli International Publications, Inc.
300 Park Avenue South
New York, NY 10010
www.rizzoliusa.com

© 2018 Covey Rise, LLC
Foreword by Chris Hastings

Associate Publisher: James Muschett
Editor-in-Chief: John Thames
Creative Director: Mary Katherine Sharman
Art Director: Virginia England
Editorial Assistant: Addy McDaniel
Copy Editors: Bowers Editorial, Molly Hammond
Photo Editor: Terry Allen

Covey Rise is a bi-monthly upland lifestyle magazine that captures the essence of the upland sporting lifestyle and is carefully crafted with extraordinary words and images. We make extra investments in the reading experience because we know that our readers enjoy the vibrant photography and narrative nuances that embody the rich traditions of our shared lifestyle.
For more information, please visit www.coveyrisemagazine.com

2018 2019 2020 2021 / 10 9 8 7 6 5 4 3 2 1

Printed in China

ISBN-13: 978-1-5996-2145-6

Library of Congress Catalog Control Number: 2018937213